D0150319

Manager's Guide to Performance Reviews

Other titles in the Briefcase Books series include:

To learn more about titles in the Briefcase Books series go to
www.briefcasebooks.com
You'll find the tables of contents, downloadable sample chapters, information on the authors, discussion guides for using these books in training programs, and more.

A Briefcase Book

Manager's Guide to Performance Reviews

Robert Bacal

McGraw-Hill

New York Chicago San Francisco Lisbon London
Madrid Mexico City Milan New Delhi San Juan
Seoul Singapore Sydney Toronto

The *McGraw·Hill* Companies

Copyright © 2004 by The McGraw-Hill Companies, Inc. All rights reserved.
Printed in the United States of America. Except as permitted under the
United States Copyright Act of 1976, no part of this publication may be
reproduced or distributed in any form or by any means, or stored in a data-
base or retrieval system, without the prior written permission of the publisher.

1 2 3 4 5 6 7 8 9 0 AGM/AGM 0 9 8 7 6 5 4 3

ISBN 0-07-142173-4

*This is a CWL Publishing Enterprises Book, developed and produced for
McGraw-Hill by CWL Publishing Enterprises, Inc., Madison, Wisconsin,
www.cwlpub.com.*

This publication is designed to provide accurate and authoritative information in regard to the subject matter covered. It is sold with the understanding
that neither the author nor the publisher is engaged in rendering legal,
accounting, or other professional service. If legal advice or other expert
assistance is required, the services of a competent professional person
should be sought.
> —*From a Declaration of Principles jointly adopted by a Committee
> of the American Bar Association and a Committee of Publishers*

McGraw-Hill books are available at special quantity discounts to use as pre-
miums and sales promotions, or for use in corporate training programs. For
more information, please write to the Director of Special Sales, McGraw-Hill,
2 Penn Plaza, New York, NY 10121-2298. Or contact your local bookstore.

This book is printed on recycled, acid-free paper containing a minimum of 50% recycled de-inked fiber.

Contents

Preface

Performance reviews seem to be a lightning rod for disappointment, dread, or even wrath on the part of employees who have to be "reviewed" and managers who feel they have to do the "reviewing." It's hard to find people who express satisfaction with their review processes, and it's not an understatement to say that, by and large, almost everyone hates them—whether getting them or giving them ... and for very good reasons.

Somehow or other, we've managed to forget what performance reviews are for, and even in situations where someone *does* remember, the process is so poorly implemented that it ends up having no value to anyone. Worse, poorly conducted performance reviews create more problems than they solve and end up costing real time and money that should be used more productively.

It's almost as if human resource departments, managers, supervisors, and employees conspire to make sure performance reviews end up as wasted effort. You couldn't mess them up more if you tried.

Most people have had poor experiences with the review process because it hasn't been implemented well. As a result, people (and this applies to managers and employees) have come to the conclusion that the performance review is a necessary evil, so they go through the motions, create a maddening paper chase, and grumble all the while. In effect, they've given up.

Of course, giving up isn't exactly the best way to improve something. So people carry on, every year repeating what they did last year and even pretending the badly executed process is valuable. In some circumstances, someone will make a sincere effort to revamp the process, and guess what? The result is a bunch of cosmetic changes that have no effect on the value of the performance review.

Here's the vicious cycle sequence. Most people have not had the chance to benefit by being involved in performance reviews that actually work. When you have unpleasant experiences with something, and had have never pleasant ones, it's not surprising that you are unable to shift your thinking in ways that will actually *help* you use the "thing" productively. You tend to believe it's useless, and it becomes that necessary evil mentioned above.

Making Performance Reviews Work

It doesn't have to be that way. It may be true that most performance reviews are wasted, but it is also true that there are many organizations, managers, and employees who are using the performance review as a tool to improve individual and organization performance, reduce managerial workload, improve employee morale, and create other benefits and advantages. They may be in the minority, but they prove that performance reviews *can* work and they *can* benefit everyone involved.

The thing is that performance reviews will work only if they are done properly. Doing them properly may mean a small shift in perspective and mindset, but that shift is one easily achieved. We also know that effective performance reviews share a number of characteristics and look different from those that are ineffective. Managers lead the meetings differently. Both managers and employees talk differently in effective performance review meetings. The communication patterns are different. Believe it or not, when reviews are done well, a lot of the pressure and unpleasantness associated with them disappears. Dread disappears.

That's where this book comes in. It's a hands-on, "as-practical-as-you-can-get" guide to making reviews work. It explains the mindset you need to review performance properly. It identifies the most common pitfalls for you to avoid. It reminds you about and teaches you how to use communication skills differently.

Above all, it brings you back to the real reason we do performance reviews. It's simple—to improve performance and create the most success for everyone, from the stockholders and shareholders right down to the backbone of your organization, the employees.

But ...

If you are looking for some way to use performance reviews to hit employees over the head or whip them into shape, you will not like this book. If you are unwilling to give up the idea that performance reviews are something done *to* employees, and not *with* them, then this book will drive you batty.

If however, you really want to reap the benefits that are possible when you review performance effectively, and you are willing to commit to the goal of *improving* performance by working with employees, you will benefit from this book.

Whether you are hoping to completely revamp your performance reviews or whether you just want to tweak them, you'll find this book full of very practical ideas. These ideas, actions, and suggestions will work only if you start with an open mind and entertain the possibility that the performance reviews can be an exceedingly powerful tool.

Special Features

The idea behind the books in the Briefcase Books Series is to give you practical information written in a friendly, person-to-person style. The chapters are relatively short, deal with tactical issues, and include lots of examples. They also feature numerous sidebars designed to give you different types of specific information. Here's a description of the boxes you'll find in this book.

These boxes do just what their name implies: give you tips and tactics for using the ideas in this book to intelligently manage the performance review process.

These boxes provide warnings for where things could go wrong when you're planning and conducting performance reviews.

These boxes give you how-to and insider hints for effectively carrying out performance reviews.

Every subject has some special jargon, including the this one dealing with performance reviews. These boxes provide definitions of these terms.

It's always useful to have examples that show how the principles in the book are applied. These boxes provide descriptions of text principles in action.

This icon identifies boxes where you'll find specific procedures you can follow to take advantage of the book's advice.

How can you make sure you won't make a mistake when conducting a performance review? You can't, but these boxes will give you practical advice on how to minimize the possibility of an error.

Acknowledgments

First and foremost, I'd like to thank Nancy who has to put up with my wacky behavior and general impatience during the writing process. Never underestimate the effort involved in the care and feeding of an author.

I would also like to thank John Woods, of CWL Publishing, and Robert Magnan, who patiently and diligently takes my impaired prose and makes it healthy.

And finally, once again, to my "other" family: Allan, Sylvia, Brian, Marty, and Chris. See you on December 24, 2025 in the old folks home. I'll send you a rattle in the morning, you old cougars! And, keep the light on, we're a'comin' home.

About the Author

Robert Bacal is CEO of Bacal & Associates, a training and consulting firm dedicated to contributing to the work success of both individual and companies, by helping managers and employees work together more effectively to create bottom line results for everyone. He holds a graduate degree in applied psychology and has been training, providing consulting services and writing on workplace issues for 25 years.

This book is his fourth on performance-related topics. He is the author of *Performance Management*, also in the Briefcase Books Series, and has authored *The Complete Idiot's Guide to Consulting* and *The Complete Idiot's Guide to Dealing with Difficult Employees* and was co-author of *Perfect Phrases for Performance Reviews*.

Robert is also an accomplished keynote speaker on performance, communication, and customer service issues; is the founder of the world's largest discussion group on performance management; and hosts a number of sites containing free resources and performance management-related tools. You can visit his main Web site at www.work911.com. His e-mail address is ceo@work911.com, and he invites comments or suggestions about any of his books.

Robert currently lives in Winnipeg, Canada, but plans a relocation to Ottawa, Canada by the end of 2003.

A Tale of Two Performance Reviews

I'd like to invite you to take part in a little detective work as we solve the mystery of the tale of two performance reviews. The sleuthing task, as it were, is to identify how it's possible for performance reviews to succeed in one context and fail miserably in another. Ready?

Let me introduce you to two managers, two companies, and two ways of reviewing performance. It's likely your situation will strongly resemble one or the other.

One Fails, One Succeeds

Jessica is a middle manager at the Aquatec Company, a manufacturing and retail chain that sells bathroom and pool supplies. She's dedicated and smart and wants to do the best job she can. Mike is also a middle manager, at another company in the same sector—Waterworks. He's also dedicated, smart, and committed. Neither is cursed with negative attitudes about employees and both share a common belief that most employees really want to do well.

Every year the managers in both companies are expected to conduct performance reviews with their staff. Jessica and Mike both schedule performance review meetings at least once a year, since that's what their companies require.

With respect to performance reviews, that's about all these two managers have in common. What they do, how they do what they do, and their experiences with performance reviews are very different. Different though they may be, both use the term "performance review" to describe what they do.

Let's start by looking at these managers' feelings about the performance review process. Managers' perceptions of performance reviews are often excellent indicators of how the performance review systems are working for them. Strong dislikes also affect how managers conduct performance reviews, and they make reviews less effective.

Jessica hates them. When I asked her if she looked forward to these meetings, she said, *"Lord, no. I'd rather crawl over broken glass than have to conduct these meetings. There are always a few employees that get really upset during the meetings and after, and quite frankly, I'm tired of having to grade staff as if they are kindergarten children."*

In response to the same question, Mike provided a completely different answer. *"Well, I find the discussions so valuable that I can't imagine not doing them. I see my job as working with staff so we all get better and keep learning, and I think my staff understands that. While there are some disagreements during review meetings, they are rarely unpleasant."*

How very strange that two people, equally bright,

Smart Managing

Self-Fulfilling Prophecy

When managers and employees dread the performance review process, two things are almost certain: the process is ineffective and the managers' negative perceptions are ensuring that it will remain ineffective. If you and your employees find the process uncomfortable, you have to look at changing the process so it *is* worthwhile. That means creating a process that's not quite so uncomfortable.

educated, and dedicated have such completely different views about the performance reviews. It's a puzzle. Maybe their employees can shed some light on the mystery.

Jessica's employees have somewhat different opinions, but there are some common threads in their responses to questions about their performance reviews. Generally, they don't quite understand the point, feel the meetings are unpleasant, and walk out feeling no better (and often much worse) than when they went into the meetings.

Mike's employees generally feel they accomplish things during the performance review meetings with Mike. For example, one of Mike's employees said it this way: *"I'm always a bit nervous before the meeting, but you know what? By the end of the meeting I feel like Mike is working with me to help me, and not to club me over the head. And I feel better able to get my job done as a result of the meetings. In fact, I think the meetings have helped me improve at my job to the point that I will probably be promoted."*

Things get curiouser and curiouser. We know now that Mike and Jessica differ in their perceptions of performance reviews and that their staffs differ in their perceptions as well. Let's take a quick look at the bigger picture. Are there differences in how the two companies see performance reviews?

We can look at this by talking to the human resources (HR) people in each company, since it's usually the HR people who are responsible for compiling the performance review paperwork as part of personnel records.

John, an HR specialist at Aquatech, didn't mince words when he was asked about performance reviews. *"It drives me nuts. I can't get the managers to do the reviews or the paperwork each year. Some employees haven't had reviews for more than five years, and I'm darned tired of nagging managers who should know better. It's not too much to ask, is it, to just fill in some simple forms once a year?"*

Mary, in HR at Waterworks, seemed to be talking about something completely different. *"Overall our managers seem to*

MISTAKE PROOFING!

Cost or Investment

If you view performance reviews as something you *have* to do and as a cost rather than an invest-ment, it's likely you are getting little value from them and your attitude and understanding of performance reviews need some tweaking. No sur-prise, really. Most of us have had bad experiences with performance reviews as employees and we bring that experience with us when we become managers.

spend the time to get the reviews done, but then again we've worked with them so they understand why it's important to do them and helped them learn to do the reviews so that everyone involved sees the advantages of doing them properly. Our position is that we care less about getting forms completed than about managers sitting down with their employees regularly to talk about how things have gone and how to make things better."

If we had access to each company's bigger picture, we'd also find differences. A cost-benefit analysis would show that the performance review program at Aquatech is "overhead," that is, the cost of doing performance reviews outweighs any return that Aquatech receives from them. For Waterworks, it's different. Its performance reviews actually contribute to the company's bottom line. Their employees improve more quickly, contribute more to the company's goals, tend to be more satis-fied with how they are treated, and tend to stay longer with the company.

The Key Questions

The question we need to ask is "How is it possible that two managers and their companies appear to be doing the same thing—performance reviews—and end up with completely dif-ferent results?" The simple answer is that the usefulness of per-formance reviews is determined by how people understand the functions, usefulness, and process of reviewing performance and how they act on their different understandings. If you were to sit in on performance reviews in both companies, you'd be struck by how different those meetings look. They're hardly alike at all.

Another important question is "Where do my company and I fit here?" Are you more like Aquatech or like Waterworks? Chances are that you are much closer to the failures at Aquatech than the successes at Waterworks. That's because more performance review systems work improperly than properly.

Should You Care?

Should you care whether your performance review process is working or not? Yes. Here's why.

Performance reviews are very powerful tools that can contribute to your personal success, the success of your employees and work unit, and the success of your company—*provided* they are done properly and the review process is carried out with the goal of improving success for everyone involved. If your performance review system is not working as well as it could, you're losing the benefits you could be getting from your system. Here are some of the benefits you lose due to poorly conducted performance reviews.

- Identifying performance difficulties early on, before they grow into large problems.
- Improving the relationships between manager and employee and creating a climate of trust.
- Putting manager and employee "on the same side," creating a climate that's not confrontational.
- Identifying barriers to performance that are not under the control of the employee but under your control.
- Identifying which employees can benefit from job training and which might be developed to take on greater responsibilities.
- Helping each employee understand how his or her job and performance contribute to the company and its success.

- Having documentation when and if it is necessary to take disciplinary or remedial action, so both you and the company are protected from unjustified legal accusations.

Real World Successes

In a 1994 study that included over 450 companies, Hewitt & Associates, concluded that companies with effective performance management systems outperformed those without on measures like employee productivity, cash flow, stock price and value, and profitability.

Perhaps a more compelling reason for caring about whether your performance reviews are effective or not lies in the consequences of having a system that is failing. Performance review systems are rarely neutral in terms of their costs and benefits. They either contribute or cause damage. It may be true that damage from poor systems is hard to find unless you're looking for it, but poor systems cause real damage to companies and to your ability to manage effectively.

Let's look at some of these hidden damages of poor systems.

- Performance review systems that don't help employees do their jobs hurt the relationships between employee and manager and create confrontational situations.
- Managers doing ineffective performance reviews lose credibility with employees, particularly when the manager acts as if the reviews are valuable when they are clearly not. Employees are smart: they know when a manager is just pretending to do something useful.
- Time and resources are lost. The only reason to justify doing performance reviews is if they somehow add value. If they don't add value, they cost.
- Poor performance review systems can make the HR staff seem amazingly stupid when the forms and mandatory requirements they set out are clearly a waste of time.

So, let's recap. What do we know so far? We know that

Jessica and Mike have very different feelings about the performance review process: Jessica hates it and Mike doesn't.
Their employees also have very different perceptions: Jessica's
employees have a strong dislike, a "'what's the point?' attitude,"
while Mike's employees, although not always perfectly comfortable, see the process as beneficial or worth the time and effort.
Comments from the two HR sections tell us similar stories.
Finally, we know that Waterworks seems to be receiving clear
and obvious bottom-line benefits from performance reviews,
while Aquatec isn't. In fact, for Aquatech, performance reviews
actually cost in time, benefits, and productivity. That brings us
to the great mystery, the real question that we need to address.
What distinguishes these two companies and these two managers from each other? That's the question we must answer if
we have any hope of improving performance reviews in our
own companies.

What Distinguishes Effective Reviews from Ineffective Reviews?

Life would be much easier if we could identify one single variable that separates good and poor performance review processes. If there were just one essential difference, then all you'd
have to do to move from poor to good would be to change that
one thing. Unfortunately, it's not like that.

Effective reviews and ineffective reviews are different in
many, many ways. If you want to improve them, you have to
address most, if not all, of the ways in which they differ. Let's
take a look at the characteristics of performance reviews that
make them more or less effective and increase or decrease the
return on investment.

Clear Primary Purpose vs. Befuddled Purpose

One of the challenges in making performance reviews work is
that people tend to try to use reviews for a number of purposes or
goals. In itself that wouldn't be a problem, except that those pur-

poses often conflict, making it impossible for a system to achieve *any* of its purposes. Performance reviews work best when the players (company, managers, and employees) clearly understand why they're doing what they're doing and when they understand that performance reviews can't achieve purposes that conflict.

Let me give you a concrete example. Many companies and managers want to use the performance review results to make personnel decisions that significantly impact employees. Since they want to reward good performance, retain top employees, make decisions on promotions, and even determine who to keep and who to let go, it's sensible to want to have data on which they can base these decisions. They look to the performance reviews to provide that data.

They may also want to use performance reviews to improve performance and to develop staff abilities. On the surface, it may appear that these two purposes are complementary, but in fact, they create conflict and put managers and employees in almost a schizoid situation.

To gather data for important personnel decisions, the responsibility for evaluating performance generally lies with the manager, not the employee. That's because the manager is the one making those important decisions. Since the employee knows the performance review information may be used to help or harm him or her, the employee doesn't perceive that it's in his or her best interests to be completely open, honest, or accurate about his or her performance. In other words, the evaluative, manager-centered performance review, tied to rewards and punishments, actually pushes the man-

> **TRICKS OF THE TRADE** **Building Trust Helps**
> There's no way to completely eliminate cross-purposes unless one decouples the performance review process from pay, reward, and punishment, something that may be problematic. I've found that managers with excellent interpersonal skills who create bonds of trust with their employees can manage this paradox well. Managers who do not have those relationships of trust face many more difficulties with the performance review process.

ager and employee to opposite sides. The employee benefits from highlighting what he or she has done well, in the hope of receiving a pay raise or not getting laid off. The tie to rewards and punishments becomes a wedge between manager and employee and keeps them from working together to improve performance.

We end up here with two purposes or functions that interfere with each other. If the goal is to make decisions about rewards and punishments, manager and employee often work at cross-purposes and take on confrontational roles. However, if the goal is to improve performance, the *only* way that will work over time is if manager and employee work together cooperatively, in partnership, within a non-threatening climate, as partners in the process.

Of all the things that distinguish effective performance reviews from ineffective, this is the toughest one to overcome. All of the ones we describe later can be fixed. This one, however, is basically a paradox, since there are legitimate reasons to use review data to make decisions and to use review data to improve performance. But you should determine what is *most* important to you and your work unit and company. Define your primary purpose and aim at it, while being aware that other purposes can creep in and cause conflicts.

Unclear vs. Clear Definition

There are currently a lot of definitions and different terms used to describe meetings where performance is discussed. For example, there are performance reviews, performance appraisals, employee reviews, and performance management, just to name a few. Some of these terms differ only slightly in meaning and some differ significantly. Believe it or not, you'll find that where performance reviews don't work well, it's often the case that people don't share a clear common definition and understanding of performance reviews. Managers and HR staff assume that people understand it the same way, but there's no guarantee that's the case. We need a definition that explains both the process and the main purpose of the performance review.

Performance review
Usually a face-to-face meeting between manager and employee to discuss the employee's performance for the purpose of removing barriers to performance. It does not stand on its own, but is intimately tied to other parts of a larger performance management process.

I recommend using performance *review* rather than performance *appraisal* or performance *evaluation* because it captures the idea of reviewing performance *together*. Here's one way of defining it. The performance review is usually a face-to-face meeting between manager and employee to discuss the employee's performance for the purpose of removing barriers to performance. It does not stand on its own, but is intimately tied to other parts of a larger performance management process.

We need to define *performance management* also, but we'll do that later on.

A definition is useless, of course, unless everyone involved understands it. Whether you use this definition or another, it's important that executives, HR staff, managers, and employees all understand it. That means communication among all of the parties.

Past vs. Future Orientations

Performance reviews tend to fail, to cost money rather than add value, when their primary focus is on what's happened in the past. The explanation is really quite simple. What's done is done. Nothing from the past can be changed. If we wish to influence performance to boost success, we need to look at the past, learn from it, and apply what we've learned to the present in order to influence the future. Someone once said, "You don't drive by looking in the rear-view mirror, so why do you manage that way?" That's a darned good question.

On the other hand, where manager and employee analyze the past to identify patterns and causes of reduced performance and work together to remove those causes in the future, performance improvement occurs. Don't dwell on the past. Use the past to inform the present.

Blaming vs. Problem Solving

Maybe it's part of human nature, but we tend to want to blame someone for things that go wrong. You see this everyday in the news, sports, interpersonal relationships, and politics: a huge percentage of the discussion on issues centers on finding fault when something goes wrong. The blaming process tries to isolate *who* is at fault.

Problem solving is different. Its major purpose is to identify *why* something went wrong, and not necessarily *who* caused the problem. On some occasions, the *who* becomes relevant, but only in terms of identifying the causes of the problem in order to fix it or prevent it from happening again. Also, blame looks backward, while problem solving centers on the present and the future. The blaming process also contains a huge emotional component. The "blamer" usually blames with anger, while the "blamee" reacts emotionally, often with anger, but also with defensiveness or trying to strike back or avoid blame.

It's probably clear to you why a focus on blame makes performance reviews ineffective. First, it creates emotional reactions in the person targeted as the one to blame. Second, blaming doesn't bring about solutions.

Forms vs. Process

Another feature that distinguishes between failed reviews and successful reviews is the emphasis: is it on completing the forms or on carrying out a productive and constructive practice? One common complaint of both managers and employees regarding performance reviews is that it seems like "one big paper chase": apart from getting forms completed, they don't see any purpose in it. Managers often set the focus on forms both before and during review meetings. If the goal of performance reviews is perceived as completing forms, it's damaging.

Doing To vs. Doing With

In looking at differences between managers who succeed with performance reviews and those who apparently do not, something else emerges. Managers who do not profit from performance reviews often believe, consciously or not, that they must *do* or *give* something *to* the employee. In other words they see their roles as evaluating, as deciding how well the employee has done. Managers who profit from performance reviews consider the review as an opportunity to *discuss* performance *with* employees.

If, for example, you could observe Mike and Jessica during their reviews with employees, you would see that Jessica does most of the talking during her sessions, while Mike does much less talking and far more questioning and encouraging the employee to self-evaluate. This is important, since it puts Mike and each employee on the same side and, even more important, it puts some evaluative and problem-solving responsibility just where it should sit—on the shoulders of the employee. Why? The employee is the only person who is there for every job task he or she performs, the constant observer of performance. The manager is not. Despite what most managers think, an employee doing a job for eight hours every day knows a lot more about the job than the manager *and* is in a far better position to solve job-related problems than anyone else. If the employee isn't allowed the opportunity to do so, a very valuable benefit of the performance review is lost.

Narrow vs. Broad Views of Performance

Ineffective performance reviews tend to focus almost entirely on what the *employee* has done and what the *employee* needs to do to improve his or her performance. That's in line with some of our cultural values that suggest that we are the masters of our fate and we control our behavior and the results of that behavior. The problem is not that these cultural values are correct or incorrect, but that they are incomplete. The behaviors of an employee, the results, and the contributions are affected by various factors, many of which are not under the control of the employee. If our goal is to improve performance, we must look at a broader spread of causes and not only at the employee. Even the most talented employee is going to have difficulty performing well if he or she lacks the tools, is impeded by poor business and production planning, is not given sufficient resources, or is adversely affected by the work environment. So, it's important—particularly when trying to determine "what went wrong" and "how to fix it"—to look broadly for causes and solutions.

Skilled Managers vs. Unskilled

Just as employees differ in terms of job skills, managers vary in terms of the job skills required to manage employees or, more specifically, to plan and conduct performance reviews. Almost anyone can sit down with an employee, tell where he or she screwed up, and threaten with punishment. We're fairly good at that. To lead a performance review that builds positive relationships and improves performance requires more advanced interpersonal, communication, and problem-solving skills. In short, it takes little skill to do something badly. It takes fairly sophisticated skills to do something well. The skills of the manager have an effect on the success or failure of the performance review process.

Generic vs. Specific Tools

There is a strong tendency for HR departments to want a consistent method for evaluating, reviewing, and documenting performance. They have some valid reasons for wanting this, at least from their perspectives, since it helps them do their jobs and makes their lives easier. Since personnel records (and usually documents related to performance

> **Dialogue—An Effective Counter**
>
> *TRICKS OF THE TRADE*
>
> If you are given generic tools to use, generic forms that you *must* use, you counterbalance them with a focus on communication and dialogue with the employee. Dialogue allows you to succeed in spite of poor tools.

reviews) end up with HR, they usually provide a standard form or set of forms for managers to use.

Since the forms are "standard," they are by necessity generic and not related specifically to any one particular job. In some cases, more sophisticated HR departments will provide different forms for managers and for janitors, for example, but nonetheless standardization is an important goal for HR departments.

The problem, though, is that a generic set of forms doesn't bring out or record information specifically enough to help managers and employees improve performance. If managers follow the form and the standard processes suggested or required by HR and do *only* the minimum (completing the form), the process becomes virtually useless. That's because general estimates of employee attitudes or skills aren't going to improve anything—although they are good at making employees angry. To improve performance, you need specifics and your employees need specifics.

As a manager, you may be working with performance review tools that are flawed and way too general. That's a good example of how *your* performance can be affected by an outside variable. The solution, apart from lobbying to improve the tools, is to go beyond them. Nobody requires you to limit your discussions during performance reviews to only what is on the form. Get specific.

Behavior/Results vs. Personality/Attitude

When you look at performance, you can look at a number of things, such as the following:

- observable behavior
- observable results
- quantifiable contributions
- personality
- attitudes

Generally we believe that people's actions are very much affected by their personalities and attitudes. I'm not going to debate the issue of whether that's accurate or, if so, to what extent. That would take a book devoted only to that subject.

What I can say is that a fast way to completely destroy the value of performance reviews is to focus too much on personality and attitude. Here's why. Most of us are a little sensitive about discussing our actions and behaviors when there's a possibility that we've done something inadequately. Discussing our attitudes or personalities, though, almost always makes us defensive, if not angry. Take a look at the following statements, all of which address personality or attitude.

- If you were more aggressive, you'd probably do better.
- Sometimes it seems like you are lazy.
- I think the fact you are so introverted and shy makes you less effective.
- People have commented on your poor attitude.

Statements like that, used in performance review meetings, are bound to cause problems. Perhaps not for everyone, but for most people. We simply don't like being judged on the basis of who we are. If we have to be judged, we're more comfortable being judged on the basis of what we've done, since that judgment is a little less personal.

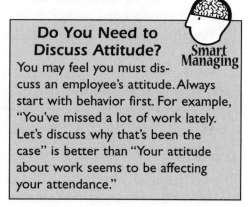

Do You Need to Discuss Attitude?

Smart Managing

You may feel you must discuss an employee's attitude. Always start with behavior first. For example, "You've missed a lot of work lately. Let's discuss why that's been the case" is better than "Your attitude about work seems to be affecting your attendance."

There's a way to address attitudes and personalities within performance reviews that's not so destructive. We'll talk in more detail about this in Chapter 11, but here's the trick: start with behavior and actions. When you ask the question, "Why did this ineffective behavior happen?" track backwards from behavior to these other, softer variables. Also, don't do the tracking yourself in this diagnostic process. You encourage the employee to do it, through appropriate questioning.

Data as Accurate and Objective vs. Data as Indicative

Particularly when people use tools that seem to measure performance in a numeric way, as we find with employee rating systems, there's a very strong natural tendency to treat those numbers or evaluations as being objective and accurate, particularly after the fact. People forget that the "data," such as ratings on a one-to-five scale, are still very subjective and do not reflect the same kind of measure as "real" numbers, like dollar sales or number of widgets produced in a month.

Real numbers are quantifiable and if you count correctly should give you the same result no matter who counts. These are objective and accurate measurements. With rating scales, that's not the case. The rating or number assigned reflects a very subjective judgment. Misuse happens and poor decisions are made when that data is considered accurate and objective. It's not. It's not accurate because it really doesn't involve measuring. It's not objective either.

Managers and companies that forget this can get into trouble. Treating any performance review data as objective and accurate when it is probably not can result in poor personnel decisions. It's best to treat all performance review data, except that determined by real quantitative measurement, as performance indicators, but *not* accurate exact measurements of performance.

Overemphasis on Manager vs. Employee

Related to earlier comments about doing to employees and working with employees, performance reviews that succeed and add value tend to emphasize the employee's input rather than the manager's. Both, of course, are important. The manager provides a sounding board for the employee and is an important source of information about how performance can be improved. However, the ultimate goal is to encourage employees to review their performance all the time. For that they need the opportunity to learn how to do it. So, if you want a performance review system that runs at maximum potential, it's good to keep in mind that you want the employee doing most of the "review work."

Integrated vs. Dangling or Disconnected

The last item that distinguishes effective performance reviews from ineffective is the degree to which those involved (executives, HR, managers, and employees) understand how performance reviews are linked to other processes in the workplace.

The awful reviews tend to be unconnected to anything important (except perhaps pay) and are seen as largely irrelevant to regular day-to-day life. They become a task viewed as an imposition and a burden, something to get out of the way, rather than a valuable tool that helps the company, manager, and employee succeed.

On the other hand, effective performance reviews are almost always linked to other things. For example, they should have links to strategic planning, tactical planning, training and development, system and production improvement, and personnel strategies. Performance reviews work within a system of performance management that includes performance planning, communication during the year, and ongoing performance problems. We're going to explain all these linkages, particularly in Chapters 2, 6, 8, 10, and 11. For now, it's enough to say that effective performance reviews need to be linked to other important processes and that all the parties understand those links. That creates meaning and perceptions that the performance reviews are, indeed, relevant to everyone.

Jessica, Mike, and You

We've explained a significant mystery here—how two managers and two companies can both have performance review systems in place and yet achieve drastically different outcomes. The reasons are, in one sense, very simple. Jessica and Aquatech, on the one hand, and Mike and Waterworks, on the other hand, have very different understandings of what performance reviews should do and how they should be done. Those different understandings affect what the managers do—and that's the key. As I said earlier, if you could sit in on the review meetings at those companies, you'd be hard pressed to identify many similarities. They are doing completely different things, but calling them by the same name.

The complexity comes from the sheer number of differences. Effective and ineffective performance reviews are different in so many ways. Consequently, to go from ineffective to effective means that most of the characteristics of poor reviews need to be altered or, if they cannot be changed, worked around.

Whether you are like Jessica or like Mike or somewhere in between, the good news is that it's possible to turn things around. You can't do it overnight, but you can do it—and you can start seeing results quickly and little-by-little improvements.

Here's a starting point for you. Use the checklist that follows to identify the barriers you need to remove to improve your performance reviews.

- Definitions are unclear and you and your employees have no common understanding.
- Reviews focus on past and not present and future.
- The emphasis is on blaming rather than solving problems.
- Reviews focus too much on the forms rather than the communication process.
- Managers dominate and control rather than share control.
- The view of performance is very narrow.
- Managers lack the skills required to conduct reviews.
- The tools are too generic and not customized.

Manager's Checklist for Chapter 1

❏ Examine how you do performance reviews now. Identify whether your reviews more closely resemble effective reviews or ineffective reviews, as outlined in this chapter.

❏ Recognize that poor performance reviews make you look foolish and ineffective to your employees and damage your credibility as a manager.

❏ Commit to the idea that the primary function of performance reviews is to improve performance—and not to find
someone to blame for actions past.

❏ Evaluate the tools you use to review performance. If they
are lacking, begin thinking how you can have them
changed and improved or how you can supplement them.

❏ Give careful thought to the idea that performance is not
completely under the control of the individual employee,
just as you don't have total control of your own performance, and that to improve performance you need to take a
wider look at what impedes individual performance.

Performance Reviews in the Scheme of Things

At this point I hope you've bought into the simple premise of this book—that performance reviews must add value to the company, to you as a manager, and to your employees. If they don't serve any function for the company, it's hard to justify doing them at all. No value, just cost. As a manager, if you can't see the value of doing them, then you won't want to do them or you won't spend the time to do them properly. Let's not forget the employees, a group we often ignore. If employees don't see value for themselves, they aren't likely to cooperate during the process.

In this chapter we're going to talk about laying the foundation so that the performance review adds value. In particular we start from the premise that by itself, and unconnected to other "things," the performance review is virtually useless or even damaging.

Reviews as Just One Part of a Larger System

In Chapter 1, I mentioned that one difference between reviews that work and reviews that don't is that effective reviews are connected to other things in the organization. They don't dangle. Here's what that means. What happens *before* the meetings and *after* the meetings is at least as important as what happens *during* the meetings. If *nothing* relevant goes on before and after, there's almost no point in doing reviews at all.

The performance review or performance review meeting is only one part of an overall strategy for improving performance that we call *performance management.* Performance management is an ongoing communication process, undertaken in partnership, between an employee and his or her immediate supervisor that involves establishing clear expectations and understanding about the following:

- The employee's essential job functions
- The ways in which the employee's performance contributes to the goals of the organization
- The meaning, in concrete terms, of "doing the job well"
- The ways in which employees and supervisors will work together to sustain, improve, or build on current employee performance
- The means of measuring job performance
- Identification of barriers to performance and actions to remove them

The performance review is just a part of the whole that is the entire performance management system. What are the other parts?

Performance management Ongoing communication process between employee and supervisor for the purpose of improving job performance and contributions. Performance management is a system. That is, it has a number of parts, *all* of which need to be included if the performance management system is to add value to the organization, managers, and employees. One of those parts is the *performance review.*

Performance Planning

Performance planning is the starting point for performance management and it is essential in laying the groundwork for effective reviews later on. Performance planning is the process of communication between manager and employee intended to create agreement about what the employee is to do, how well he or she needs to do it, and why, when, and how success is to be determined.

Key Term

Performance planning A process of communication between manager and employee so both are clear on what the employee is expected to do or achieve in the coming year and how success is to be determined.

Performance management starts here. When each employee has goals that he or she and the supervisor understand completely and in the same way, it's more likely that the employee will succeed. It's the achievement of these goals that's going to form the basis for the performance review later in the year. In other words, first you plan for performance by setting the targets for the coming period/year; then, you use the performance review to examine whether the employee met those goals and make sure any problems are addressed.

Imagine you and your family are going on a trip. You get the kids ready, make sure there are enough toys to keep the kids sane (you hope!), make sure the car (these days it's probably an SUV) is mechanically sound, and hit the open highway. You drive eight hours the first day and stop at a motel. In the morning you set out again and, at the end of the day, stop at another motel. After dinner you convene a family meeting where you review the trip. "So," you might ask, "have we had a good time?" Another useful question might be "Did we get to where we wanted to go?" Think of it as an informal performance review of the trip.

Unfortunately, it doesn't make a lot of sense to ask these questions and expect useful responses, because you and your family didn't do any planning. You had no goal or destination.

There wasn't even a common understanding of the purpose for the trip. Was it to attend favorite Aunt Sarah's funeral in New Jersey? Was it a vacation to the beach? Was it to scout out a town you might want to relocate to? Obviously, you can't decide whether the trip was useful or achieved its goals, if you didn't set any goals and nobody knew why you were making the trip.

The lack of planning prevents you not only from answering questions about how well the trip went, but also from asking the right questions. If the point of the trip was to go to Aunt Sarah's funeral, then you might ask, "Do you think we helped nieces Nancy and Rebecca through a tough time?" You wouldn't ask, "Well, did we all have a good time and win money at the casinos?"

Proper performance planning is the bedrock of any review. Unless you first determine your goal, you can't know if you got to where you intended to go and you certainly can't know why not.

> **Don't Skip Performance Planning**
>
> ⚠️ **CAUTION!**
>
> Some review systems and forms are set up so that you can complete them without having done any performance planning at all. For example, rating systems can be completed without any planning. Regardless of whether your formal review system requires performance planning or not, *do it!* Don't let the forms dictate.

There's one more element to the performance planning process. Both manager and employee must share a common understanding of what's expected. If you look to our travel metaphor, imagine how the "trip review" meeting would go if each member of your family had a completely different idea of the purpose for the trip. Most probably, your meeting would be chaotic and cause frustration and anger. Your teenager wouldn't agree with your six-year-old and you might not agree with your spouse. It's the same with performance reviews.

Ongoing Performance Communication

If you look at performance reviews and how they are often used in the workplace, you come across a startling, scary phenomenon. Many, if not most, managers and HR departments see the performance review as a once-a-year event. It's "something to get out of the way so real work can get done." This view and the resulting behavior virtually guarantee that the performance review meetings will fail miserably and ensure that there will be a lot of bad feelings associated with the meetings. Why?

Jessica in Chapter 1 is the prototypical manager who sets up performance reviews so they fail. We identified some of the things she does to destroy any value they might have, but let's consider one more thing.

Every year, once a year, Jessica meets with Freddy, one of her staff. Now, Freddy has always "come out OK" from the meetings. This year, in the annual meeting, Jessica says to Freddy, "Freddy, I'm sorry to say that your performance this past year has been horrible and, if it doesn't improve in the next three months, we're going to have to let you go." How do you think Freddy is going to react to this bolt of lightning?

Of course Freddy will be upset because, for all intents and purposes, he's been shanghaied. After he gets over his shock, if he doesn't do anything stupid, one of his questions is going to be "Why the hell didn't you tell me earlier?" A very good question!

Surprising Freddy this way is certainly going to make the meeting exceedingly unpleasant. It also calls into question Jessica's motives. If Jessica is interested in helping Freddy succeed, than doesn't it make sense to bring up the performance issues much earlier in the year and work with him so he can improve? If, however, Jessica's motive is to get rid of Freddy, then it makes sense to not tell him until the performance review, so he has less chance to fix things.

We can't know Jessica's motives, but one thing is sure. By dropping this bomb, she's destroyed any trust or positive relationship she might have had with Freddy. That's bad enough, but she has also damaged her relationships with all her staff. This is *not* going to remain a secret: Jessica's other employees are going to know.

Performance reviews done in the absence of ongoing communication about performance throughout the entire year cost big time. Ongoing performance communication is a two-way process throughout the year to ensure that job tasks stay on track, that problems are red-flagged before they grow, and that both manager and employee keep current.

Ongoing communication isn't just to build and maintain good relationships between manager and employee. It might be that that is the least important part of the process.

In terms of the success of the company, the work unit and the manager, the most important function of ongoing communication is to help identify problems early so they can be addressed early.

> ### A Continuous Process
>
> Thinking of performance reviews as annual events invites problems. You can avoid many of those problems through ongoing performance communication, which involves manager and employee in discussion and dialogue to keep performance on track and to identify problems early on so they can be addressed as soon as possible. It occurs all year round as needed—and it's always needed all year around.

Let's look at Freddy again. Assuming that his performance has dropped significantly during the past year, the company and the work unit have suffered from the performance deficits for a complete year. Maybe they've lost sales or customers. Maybe the quality of their products has declined. Maybe new product ideas have dried up. Whatever Freddy was expected to be accomplishing, his poor performance has hurt. Even if Freddy cleans up his act in the upcoming year, whatever was lost is lost forever. That's not a "touchy-feely" loss. That's a bottom-line financial loss that can never be recouped.

Contrast this result with how this situation is handled by Mike, our excellent performance reviewer. Early in the year, Mike notices some things that hinted at problems with Freddy's performance. While Jessica felt she was too busy to watch over employees, Mike felt it was important to keep at least one eye on things during the year. Rather than waiting until the end of the year, he intervened. Equipped with some observations about Freddy's behavior, he talked with Freddy, or rather led a discussion with Freddy about performance. It turned out that Freddy was having some family problems. Mike and Freddy worked together to ensure Freddy got the help he needed and, within a few weeks, Freddy's work started to return to his previous levels.

TRICKS OF THE TRADE

Communication Yields Flexibility

Ongoing communication during the year also allows shifting gears and changing the parameters of an employee's job when it is required. Details of performance expectations can be changed. Performance plans can be revisited. This creates a continuous feedback loop so it's possible to respond quickly to changes in the environment.

Do you see the difference? Since Mike paid attention and acted quickly, losses to the company and work unit were minimized. A side benefit was that Freddy very much appreciated Mike's help and other employees heard of Mike's efforts. The result: better relationships all around.

Ongoing performance communication can be summed up in a single, simple two-word phrase—*no surprises!* By the time the performance review rolls around, the employee should pretty much anticipate the outcomes of that meeting. Also, there should be no surprises for the manager. Any problems that arose during the year should have been identified and discussed at the time. Solutions might already be in place.

Gathering Data, Observing, and Documenting

The next component of the performance management system is gathering data, observing, and documenting. As part of an effective performance management system, all three activities can occur anytime during the year. Data gathering and observation are done during the year, outside the performance review meeting; documenting happens during the year *and* during and after the performance review meeting.

If we are going to discuss performance during performance review meetings, we can't do that in a vacuum. To be most effective, performance discussions need data and substance. For example, it's one thing to say, "Your performance is poor" and a completely different thing to say, "Last month, your production figures were down by 20% and I think we need to talk about that." The difference is huge.

Discussions based on vague judgments are guaranteed to create bad feelings and, even more important, are not specific enough to help employees improve. Gathering data and observing behavior and the consequences help keep discussions focused on more concrete and specific aspects of performance. That in turn makes it possible to work together to identify the why's of performance—why performance may have been less than desired *or* why performance improved. The latter is important so both you and the employee know what worked, so it can be repeated.

Also gathering data, observing, and documenting what you've observed help you identify problems early on—provided you are doing these things throughout the year.

Let's explain the meanings of "observing," "collecting data," and "documenting." *Observing* refers to what you have seen or heard directly that relates to an employee's performance. Observations may be based on an employee's actual observable behavior. For example, in a call center, monitoring calls would be observing. In sales, it might be listening to how the employee works with customers. Another example: seeing how an employee interacts with team members at meetings. Observations can also be based on the results or consequences of an employee's behavior. For example, you might observe that at a team meeting, several members got upset when the employee used certain sexist phrases. You observe the behavior *and* you observe the effects of that

> **Observing** The process of seeing or hearing or otherwise noting employee behavior and actions and/or the results of those actions.

Key Term

behavior on others. Both behaviors and consequences/results are part of your observations.

Collecting data is a little bit different. Information exists in the workplace that can indicate whether an employee is doing badly or well. That information may be in the form of data. Here are some examples:

- Dollar value of sales by the employee
- Number of complaints about the employee
- Number of customer commendations
- Days absent
- Number of creative ideas generated and implemented

This information can be extremely valuable during the performance review meetings. "Hard" data is less colored by opinion; it's not completely objective but it's better than vague comments. Therefore, it's a little less volatile to talk about number of days absent then to talk about the employee's attitude.

Key Term

Collecting data A process of seeking out information/data related to an employee's performance, preferably in as concrete and objective a way as possible, during the year.

You should collect data throughout the year, as an ongoing process, and not just a task just prior to a performance review meeting. It spreads the load a little bit and it allows you to identify problems during the year when it's not too late to remedy them. It's also fairer to the employee, because the data represents the entire year and not just a short time that may not be representative of the year.

Documentation is simply the recording of information about the employee's performance. That happens during the year, as needed, and as a result of the interactions between you and the employee during the performance review meeting. When documentation is done throughout the year, the primary purpose is to record important information so it won't be lost or forgotten. For example, you might observe a customer-employee interaction that went badly. Apart from dealing with it as soon as possible, you might also want to make a few notes so you can discuss the incident with the employee later on, without having to rely completely on memory.

Documentation based on the performance review meeting provides a summary, on paper, of the discussions, conclusions, and action plans that are decided upon in that meeting. Usually, they are kept permanently in an employee's personnel file.

Performance Review Meetings

Performance review meetings refer to meetings between manager and employee for the purpose of communicating and reviewing performance. It's common for these meetings to result in some sort of evaluation or appraisal, which is related to the performance review, but different.

Evaluation (or appraisal) of performance focuses on how well or how badly the employee has done. Because evaluations are usually undertaken for the purposes of rewarding and punishing employees, they tend to put manager and employee on different sides of the table.

A performance review, while it may have an evaluative component, is focused on improving performance regardless of the current levels of performance. It's a problem-solving process that puts employee and manager on the same side.

The distinction gets fuzzy in real life, of course. You can use appraisals to improve performance and you can include appraisals as part of performance reviews, but it's important to pay attention to the different focus and purposes. I firmly believe we should stop using terms like "performance appraisal" and "employee evaluation" and instead use "performance review" to reflect a way of looking at performance that is intended to add value to the company because it helps managers and employees improve performance over time.

Since this book is about conducting effective performance reviews, you'll find in subsequent chapters a lot more detail about the process and how to make reviews work. One final

CAUTION!

Once-a-Year Syndrome

The performance review is a tool to improve performance. Don't get locked into thinking of reviews as a once-a-year event, since you may find you gain more by having them more often. You need to decide how often based on some reasonable cost-benefit estimate.

point: there's a tendency to think about performance reviews as a "once-a-year event"—and that's not the case. In fact it's quite possible to have review meetings at any time. Some managers have short, five-minute performance review mini-meetings once a month.

Performance Diagnosis and Problem Solving

Let's recap where we are in the overall performance management process. We started with performance planning, working with the employee to clarify job roles, responsibilities, and expectations. We communicated all throughout the year about performance, so we could catch problems early and so there would be no surprises during the review meeting. We gathered information and made some observations of the employee's performance, again throughout the year, and we reviewed performance with the employee.

None of that has any value unless we can somehow use this process to improve performance. We've talked and clarified and now we need to move closer and closer to creating a plan of action to improve performance, regardless of the current levels.

Performance diagnosis and performance problem solving are the missing link between talking about performance and improving it.

Performance diagnosis is the process by which you work with the employee, applying information to identify the underlying causes of poor performance and reasons why performance has been good and to identify barriers to better performance in the future. Clearly, unless you know the *why's* of performance you can't develop a plan to remedy or improve it. You can't even figure out how to maintain existing performance when it is at a high level.

> **Performance diagnosis** The process of working with an employee to discover the *why's* of performance. It results in answers to questions like these:
> - "Why is your performance declining?"
> - "What barriers have you been hitting that are affecting your performance?"
> - "Why has your performance improved this year?"

When does performance diagnosis happen? It should be a major part of the performance review meeting, but if that's the only time you apply the diagnostic process, you're going to be less effective. It's also a year-round process, as is its companion, performance problem solving.

Performance problem solving is the process by which you identify and create a strategy—an action plan, if you like, to address and remove the barriers to performance you identified using performance diagnosis. Or, on the positive side, it may simply be to identify the actions you want the employee to continue, since they have been successful. Again, let's not focus *only* on what's not gone well. Yes, we need to fix problems, but we also need to know what's going well, so it can continue to go well.

By the end of performance diagnosis and performance problem solving, regardless of whether it's part of the review meeting or not, you should end up with a set of actions that you, the employee, the work unit, and/or the company are going to undertake. If your diagnosis and problem-solving outcomes are accurate, you *will* end up with better performance.

Here's an example. During the performance review, Mike, the manager, and Bob, a salesperson,

> **For One and for All**
> **Smart Managing**
> When you diagnose a problem with an employee and formulate a successful plan of action to remove a barrier, you will often find that the same issues apply to others who do similar jobs. So, this process not only can help you to improve the performance of the one employee, but also can provide insights and information that you can often apply to improve the performance of many employees.

went over some of the yearly sales figures and found that Bob was doing well selling to customers whose first language was English but was making virtually no sales with those whose mother tongue was Spanish. During the diagnostic discussion, Bob and Mike decided that Bob's inexperience with the culture and language of a major group of customers negatively affected his ability to work with them. (That's the diagnostic part.) They agreed that it might help if Bob did two things: first, learn more about the Hispanic culture and Hispanic customers, and second, take some basic Spanish lessons. The idea was to show potential customers that Bob (and the company) valued their business enough to try to speak their language. The result was that Bob's sales figures rose in that demographic. The company decided to follow similar strategies with some of its other staff members who expressed an interest.

This is a great example of how the diagnostic and problem-solving process can work. Not only can it succeed in improving one individual's performance, but also the ideas generated can be used to improve the performances of others.

Action and Following Through on Commitments

It's easy to take for granted that any plans and commitments emerging from the performance review and diagnostic process are going to be implemented—that there will be follow-through and follow-up. It's dangerous to make that assumption. If, for whatever reasons, those plans and commitments do not turn into actions, the whole value of the process is lost. After all, we don't do performance management for the fun of it or to have a fine old chat.

So the last component of the performance management process is to follow up and follow through. That means checking to make sure commitments are being kept and to monitor progress of the implementation plans.

In the example above, Mike and Bob agreed to meet again a month after the review/diagnostic meeting to discuss their progress. At that meeting, Mike indicated he'd gotten approval from the company to pay for the language lessons and seminar on Hispanic culture and history and Bob reported on various sources for training. At that point they agreed on everything and they proceeded to implement the plan. Also, at the meeting Bob came up with another suggestion—to pair with a Hispanic employee who would serve as a mentor. So, they set that up. Periodically, they'd talk informally about how things were going (ongoing communication).

Summing Up

You may have noticed that the overall performance management process we described isn't linear. The steps aren't neat and ordered. There's overlap. For example, diagnosing performance is usually part of the performance review meeting, but it's also something that can stand alone. A lock-stepped mechanical process for managing performance isn't a good idea: it's not flexible enough. If you keep in mind the purpose—to improve performance—and don't get locked into inflexible rules, you'll do far better. The exception to this is this rule: to benefit from the process, you have to do *all* of the steps.

Other Linkages

Now that you have a sense of how the performance review works as part of the performance management system, let's look at how the performance management system fits in with other things that go on in your organization. We certainly don't want performance reviews to dangle, unconnected to the related steps of performance management, since they would lose their value. Similarly, the performance management system shouldn't dangle either. By understanding how it connects to the other things the organization does, you can maximize the value of the entire process.

One thing you will notice about the rest of this chapter is that it doesn't discuss the linkages between performance review and pay, promotion, reward, and punishment. There's a reason for this. Performance reviews work best when they are not linked to rewards and punishment. I also recognize that it's likely (and even sensible) that they *are* linked in your company. Not to worry. The use of performance management and performance reviews to make personnel and salary decisions will be discussed in detail later in the book.

Strategic Planning and Unit/Company Goals

Are you comfortable with the idea that an employee's true value is related to how well he or she contributes to the goals of the work unit and the company? You should be.

Believe it or not, it's not uncommon for employees to be low contributors because their jobs and responsibilities have not been carefully planned and "rationalized" in terms of the work unit's goals. Theoretically, everything an employee does should result in a contribution.

The link between the unit/company goals and performance management is important. In a well-functioning company, here's how it works. The company has goals, targets, and so on for the upcoming year and for several years beyond that. Your work unit's goals should map out what and how the unit is to contribute toward achieving the company goals. Then it cascades down. Each employee's performance goals and responsibilities are derived from those of the work unit.

TRICKS OF THE TRADE

From Unit Goals to Employee Goals

When establishing goals for an employee, the starting point should be the goals of the work unit, to orient and align the smaller goals with the larger goals, so that if the employee achieves his or her goals, by necessity the employee is contributing to the goals of the work unit.

The linkage is forged during the performance-planning phase of performance management. That's why it's so important to put the employee's work in the context of the work and goals of the work unit. Do that and you start to maximize individual contributions.

Training, Development, and Succession Planning

How do you decide how to allocate money and resources to the training and development of your staff? In many companies, decisions about training and development are made without any rational rhyme or reason. Sometimes, training is arranged when there is a budget surplus you need to get rid of. Other times, employees make a request when they see a need and the request is approved or rejected based on very fuzzy criteria. When there's no way of determining what training is needed and who should receive it, training budgets end up wasted. Like performance reviews, the purpose of training and developing employees is so they can increase their contributions to the company. Without some sort of links to the company's goals, the work unit's goals, and the performance levels and job tasks of employees, you're wasting money.

How should you decide on allocating training and development resources? By using the information and analyses you create with each employee during the review meetings to determine how best to improve performance. The results of the reviews drive the decision-making process.

Anticipate Needs
When planning for training and development, look at past and present performance and anticipate what the employee might need to cope with a changing environment in the future. Training and development should reflect what will be needed in the future, even if it is not needed right now.

Once you've identified barriers to performance or opportunities to improve performance and you understand why they exist, you investigate whether the causes of the barriers could be remedied through training and development. If so, then you allocate resources. If, however, the true causes of the performance deficit cannot be addressed through training, then you don't allocate resources to it.

Budgeting and Spending

The performance review and larger performance management process can and should be used to make decisions about budgeting and spending. It's rather amazing that it usually isn't used to make financial decisions. As a result, performance management loses some of its potential value.

Before we look at the link between budgeting and spending and performance management and review, here's a brief, commonsense look at the financial functions. It's a bit simplified, but for our purposes it works. When you budget or spend money, you want to maximize the benefits from spending. Not only do you want the best value when you purchase something, but you also want to have it contribute to whatever goals you may have related to the purchase. In well-run organizations, budgets are decided and spending is approved based on the need for the expenditure and the value of the expenditure with respect to the organization's goals. So, the organization may pay for training with the expectation that better trained employees will perform more effectively.

Now the question: how do you know whether a particular purchase or expenditure will actually help your company achieve its goals? Sometimes you guess. Sometimes you may feel you "just know." Or, you decide on expenditures based on an analysis of your present, past, and future goals.

Here's the link. When you focus on identifying performance barriers, diagnosing performance issues, and developing plans to overcome those barriers, you can use that

Smart Managing

Finding Unnecessary Expenditures
When you begin to link performance management and review to expenditures, you might be quite surprised at the number of expenditures that really have no reason, almost no potential to improve overall performance. One common example is updating computers. Quite frequently companies do that and receive no additional value, since their current computers are quite capable of handling the workloads. Finding cases like this is managing smart.

information to decide on what you need to purchase. It's a method of tying expenditures to productivity, beginning at the bottom of the organization.

For example, during performance reviews with your staff, you identify some production problems. Several of your staff are under-performing in their job tasks. In discussions with these staff members (and others as well), you discover that the *reason* that productivity is less than maximal is that some of the tools available are no longer state-of-the-art. If that diagnosis is accurate, it's clear that to solve the problem, you need to purchase new equipment. Of course those purchases need to be planned with respect to other corporate issues. The performance review and problem-solving process tells you about how you can best spend your available resources.

Manager's Checklist for Chapter 2

❑ The performance review becomes useless if it is not connected to the other steps in the performance management process.

❑ Pay special attention to what goes on outside the review meetings. In particular, by investing time up front in performance planning, you will generate more benefit from the review meetings and keep them shorter.

❑ Live by the credo of "no surprises in reviews."

❑ Make sure you have effective communication with your staff throughout the year. That way you not only prevent surprises, but also catch problems before it's too late.

❑ You can use the information you collect in the performance management process to make more effective decisions about training, development, budgeting, and spending.

Understanding Performance— Good and Bad

L et's restate a key point. The real value of the performance review comes from its function as a communication vehicle for manager and employee to identify barriers to performance and develop plans to eliminate or overcome those barriers. Its major purpose is to help everyone succeed to the extent possible, so that the employee, the manager, and the company all benefit.

Can you use performance reviews for other things? Yes. Will you do so? Probably. Still, if you don't use the review process to improve performance, then it becomes a cost and not an asset.

One of the reasons performance reviews end up ineffective and disliked by all is that managers leading the process apply an inaccurate idea of performance and what causes it. It sounds funny, when you think about it. Performance seems like a very simple concept. How can people get it wrong?

Many managers believe that performance, good or bad, is totally under the control of the individual employee. If you start from this assumption about employee control, it's only logical that you review performance as if the employee is responsible for the good stuff and to blame for the bad stuff. While that's intuitively sensible, it's inaccurate. We'll explain why later in the chapter.

Apart from being inaccurate, this assumption pushes the performance

> **Performance** The degree to which an employee contributes to the goals of his or her work unit and company as a result of his or her behavior and the application of skills, abilities, and knowledge.

review process into a situation in which the manager is doing something *to* the employee, usually evaluating him or her, rather than encouraging a situation where the manager and the employee work as partners in problem solving. In an atmosphere of managers evaluating employees, employees tend to be uncooperative and defensive and managers feel awkward.

If you are going to maximize the benefits or value of performance reviews, you need to examine your own understanding of performance, and what contributes to good performance and bad. After all, if we want to review performance, we really need to understand it.

What Do We Mean by "Performance"?

Common sense tells us that if an employee does his or her job tasks well, he or she is "performing well." If an employee doesn't do the job tasks well, then she or he is a "poor performer." Well, that may be the perception of many, but it's way too simplistic. While you can equate performance with doing the tasks of the job, let's look at it a bit differently.

An employee is performing well when his or her actions and behaviors contribute to the goals of the company and the work unit. In this respect, we aren't looking at work performance as we would look at an athlete's performance in, for example, running the mile. We evaluate the runner's performance by looking at how long he took to run the mile or whether she was faster than everyone else, but we do *not* look at whether the running performance contributed to anything larger than the runner. At least not any more.

We might have in the past. If you recall some of your ancient history, you might remember that distance runners were used so generals in war could communicate with each other, absent our current technologies. In those roles, the runners had to run fast, but running fast wasn't the point. The point was to get messages to the generals so they could win battles.

Employees are not like modern athletes. Our main concern with work performance should not be doing well or poorly, but rather about contributing. How much does it contribute? Can it contribute better? How can we improve contributions?

> **⚠ CAUTION!**
>
> ### Narrow Focus, Poor Result
>
> The most common reason performance reviews end up as a waste of time is that the manager focuses *only* on the employee and his or her talents and actions, rather than looking at other factors essential for superior performance.

While the ability to do job tasks is important, performance itself is a much bigger issue. When you grasp the concept of performance as contribution, you have the opportunity to manage in a completely different way and to review performance in a way that involves partnering and working together.

An Example

Let's look at an example that clarifies this broader view of performance. Mary, Joan, and Mark work in a call center that handles calls from customers wanting help with a particular software product. The economics of call centers are such that employees are often evaluated on the number of customers they can deal with in a given period of time. Companies tend to view support call centers as overhead or "cost" items, since they don't generate visible income, and they tend to understaff them.

Mary is the speed demon of the department. She talks fast, thinks fast, and knows her stuff. Her throughput is the highest in the department. Joan also knows her stuff, but works more slowly, thinks more slowly, talks at a more normal and natural speed. Her throughput is a little below the average. Mark is not very knowledgeable, but oddly enough he also has a fairly high throughput and customers he deals with don't generally call back.

If we look at performance as the ability to do the primary job task (getting callers off the phone) quickly, then we'd conclude that Mary is best, Mark is second, and Joan is the least able performer, based on the average time spent on each customer call.

But what about their contributions? If we define performance as the degree to which the employee contributes to the goals of the company and work unit, we end up with a different conclusion.

The reason Mark deals with customer problems quickly and his customers don't call back is that he's no help at all. They don't call back because they've given up on him and on the company and they're going to be quite vocal about their dissatisfaction. He may be fast, but he's not contributing.

Mary, on the other hand, has a lot to offer to her customers, but she is *so* fast and so abrupt and task-oriented that she doesn't check that the customers understand her instructions before she ends the conversations. The result is that they often have to call back. Her speed is a double-edged sword: it cuts down on the length of calls but hurts customer service.

Joan, on the other hand, is the real performer. She solves 95% of customers' problems on the first call and within five minutes, while presenting a very positive image of the company. She's not just a software support consultant. She's a public relations expert as well.

You can apply the same concept of performance to sports figures. A

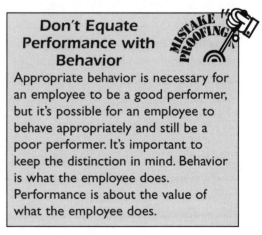

Don't Equate Performance with Behavior

Appropriate behavior is necessary for an employee to be a good performer, but it's possible for an employee to behave appropriately and still be a poor performer. It's important to keep the distinction in mind. Behavior is what the employee does. Performance is about the value of what the employee does.

baseball player hits 70 home runs in a season, but his team finishes last. Is he a high performer or not? It all depends on how you treat performance. If he has contributed to some goals important to the team (such as increasing attendance and revenue), then the answer is yes. If the team finished last and had a drop in attendance, it's likely his value to the team, economically, will be negative. That situation will probably not occur in your workplace, because the reward systems are different than in baseball, but the principle is the same. We want contributors, employees who provide value to the company.

The Stuff of Performance—Good and Poor

Your goal as a manager is to improve the performance of every staff member and the overall performance of your work unit. The performance review is one of the tools you need to reach that goal. In order to use the review as an effective tool, you need to understand where performance comes from. How does good performance happen and, perhaps more importantly, how does bad performance happen?

Employee Variables

Performance reviews as you have probably experienced them focus on employee behavior, skills, ability, knowledge, and attitudes. It's intuitively sensible that an employee who is performing well is somehow different from one who is performing less well. Take a look at the forms you currently use to "review" performance: every item listed there, no matter what kind of form, is going to be an employee variable. That reflects the importance we place on the individual employee and his or her characteristics. Here are some examples of these characteristics:

- Completes task quickly (employee speed)
- Knowledgeable about product line (employee knowledge)
- Always on time (employee habits)
- Interacts well with others (employee interpersonal skills)
- Demonstrates excellent team leadership skills (employee leadership skills)

You get the idea. There are hundreds, perhaps thousands of these employee characteristics used every day to evaluate and review employee performance. So, to sum up the issue, superior employee performance is *partly* a result of the employee behaving differently than the poor performer and possessing superior attitudes, skills, abilities, and knowledge. Individual characteristics or variables are only one contributor to performance.

System Variables

In the performance review systems that you are most familiar with, employee variables are treated as the *only* determinants of good and poor performance. That's not so. Focusing only on employee variables almost guarantees that the performance review is going to be less effective in improving both individual performance and work unit/company performance. If we want to improve performance, we need to look at both the employee and the system within which he or she works.

What are system variables or system characteristics? System variables refer to the larger environment in which each employee works. They include processes and procedures within the workplace, and the tools supplied to the employee.

> **Key Term**
>
> **System variables** Factors outside of the employee and usually not under his or her direct control. They are very powerful determinants of employee performance. They include resources, tools, management behavior, policies, and other employees.

Here's a quick list of possibilities. Notice that none of these are under the direct control of the employee.

- Skill of manager and managerial style
- Available budget
- Quality and appropriateness of tools
- Training to use the tools
- Behavior of coworkers
- Administrative policies and procedures (e.g., red tape)
- Design of work flows

- Customer expectations
- Marketing strategies
- Overall company planning

Before we look at some examples, here's a key point. System variables are *not* under the direct control of the individual employee. They are the givens in the work environment. Some of these factors are under your control as manager. Some may be under the control of other departments (e.g., the human resources department), while others may be controlled by senior executives. There may even be some that are not controlled by anyone in your organization, such as changes in the economy or customer demands.

Let's look at some examples of how system variables affect performance. Let's take two automobile repair shops.

The Acme Repair Shop is owned and operated by a skinflint who doesn't believe in any of the "newfangled" diagnostic tools. I guess you'd call the owner someone from the old school. Luckily, the mechanics working for Acme are really topnotch. They are experienced and have good logical and diagnostic skills and excellent mechanical skills.

The Golden Auto Repair Company works a bit differently. The owner has invested in the newest technology to help his mechanics do the job. As new tools become available, he decides whether to purchase them and, if so, he makes sure his mechanics receive proper training for using them. The mechanics at Golden Auto Repair are competent, but probably not excellent by any standards. The best way to describe them would be "average."

We need to ask the question, "How do the mechanics in these two companies perform or contribute to their respective company's goals?" The mechanics at Golden, although generally not possessing any above-average skills and abilities (individual variables), actually contribute much more than the excellent mechanics at Acme. A system variable—tools and training—allows average mechanics to outperform more highly skilled counterparts. The effects of system variables are very powerful.

Let's look at another, less obvious example. Jackie is head of the creative section of an ad agency that produces radio commercials. Her staff consists of five exceedingly creative people who create the ad concepts, write the scripts, and hire the "talking heads" to do the commercials. Before being promoted to section head, Jackie was one of the best creative talents around. Being used to controlling her own campaigns and excelling at the process, Jackie as manager wants to be involved in every project her employees undertake. She insists on approving every detail of each project and severely limits the decision-making authority of her employees. You're probably familiar with the term *micromanagement*, which means an attempt to manage every little detail. That's Jackie.

So, how well do her employees perform? Not so well. Since Jackie has to approve every small step, there are delays in the development of every single campaign. Jackie might believe that the resulting cost overruns and dissatisfied customers are a result of poor employee performance, but it's not. They're a result of a system variable, Jackie's own behavior.

Imagine what happens when Jackie does her annual performance reviews with her staff. From where she sits, her employees are under-performing, since what she sees are the cost overruns on the projects. If she focuses *only* on employee variables (skills, abilities, knowledge, and behavior),

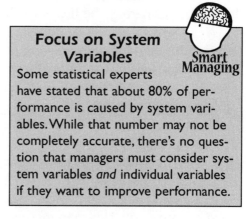

Focus on System Variables

Smart Managing

Some statistical experts have stated that about 80% of performance is caused by system variables. While that number may not be completely accurate, there's no question that managers must consider system variables *and* individual variables if they want to improve performance.

the only conclusion is that her staff members not doing their jobs. That conclusion is clearly wrong—and any actions she takes predicated on that faulty conclusion are going to be harmful if not disastrous.

Interaction of Individual and System Variables

In this chapter I've pointed out how important it is to look at system variables as they affect individual performance. So, you may be asking, "If system variables are so powerful in determining individual employee performance, why do the 10 employees who report to me, who all work in the exact same environment, perform at such different levels?"

That's a great question. The answer will help you better understand individual performance, which is after all, the focus of performance reviews.

Rather than answering the question outright, consider the situation of marathon runners. Marathons are held all over the world. In particular, the Olympic games move around, taking place sometimes in hot climates, sometimes in cooler climates, sometimes at high altitudes, and sometimes at lower ones. Those factors—systems/environmental variables—are going to affect the performance of the athletes. So, it's fair to assume that the average performance in a marathon in Mexico City (high altitude, very hot) is going to be lower than in a marathon at a lower altitude in a cooler locale. That's the *average* performance. Generally the times will be longer.

Now here's the interesting thing. Some runners will be less affected by the high altitudes and heat in the marathon in Mexico City. Perhaps because they've lived all their lives in similar environments or trained more effectively, they will not be as affected as other runners.

This interaction of individual characteristics and systems characteristics explains why we can have exceedingly varied performance in the same environment that is *not* a direct result of individual characteristics.

Let's apply this to the earlier example of Jackie and the creative ad company. Her management style impedes the effectiveness of all her staff in one way or another, but some employees are affected less than others. Let's take Bob. Bob's a creative guy who's always taken the position that it's always better to ask for forgiveness after the fact than for permission in advance. So, even though Jackie insists on approving everything, Bob presents his ideas to the client first. Once the client is happy, Bob then sends the ideas to Jackie for approval *after* the fact. While Jackie gets annoyed sometimes, Bob is pleasing his customers so Jackie is not prepared to do much about it. As a result, Bob gets things done faster than his colleagues who abide by Jackie's rules.

> **Faulty Conclusions**
> The interaction between system and individual can make some employees seem less skilled and less capable than others. If you remove some of the system variables that impede performance for those individuals, you may find that they are much more competent than you thought.

This doesn't mean Bob is more creative or even better at customer relations. It just means that in this specific system or environment, Bob is able to perform better than his peers: he is simply less affected by the system's barriers. If you change the system variables, he might appear to perform less well relative to his peers.

Implications for Your Performance Reviews

The most important implication for conducting performance reviews is this: if your goal is to improve performance and the ability of your employees to contribute to the company goals and the goals of your work unit, you *must* pay attention to barriers to performance that originate with the employee and the system in which the employee works. You also need to be aware that the system and the employee interact to produce performance, so that employees in the same job who are equally skilled may produce differently because the system variables affect each of them differently.

There are some other important implications to consider. Since performance is about contribution and not just behavior, you need to conduct your performance reviews by talking about both the employee's performance and contributions *and* the behaviors the employee exhibits to deliver that performance and make those contributions. Figure 3-1 is a very simple diagram to remind you of how the elements are interrelated.

Employee Variables	**System Variables**
Attitudes	*Tools*
Skills	*Resources*
Knowledge	*Social System*
Abilities	*Coworkers*
	Managerial Behavior
Employee variables are characteristics of the individual. You cannot see them directly: you can't open someone's head to see if he or she has good skills. The only way you can infer these variables is through performance.	System variables combine with employee variables to determine employee behavior.

Employee Behavior

Employee behavior is observable and usually measurable. Appropriate employee behavior is necessary if he or she is going to contribute, but it's possible for an employee to do what he or she is asked to do but not perform (or contribute) well.

Performance

Performance is the employee's contribution to the achievement of the goals of the company and the work unit.

Figure 3-1. Relationship of individual variables, system variables, behavior, and performance

If you're using performance review information to determine promotions and whether an employee will be retained or let go, keep in mind that each employee's performance is influenced by his or her own skills and abilities, but also strongly affected by the system in which he or she works. Sometimes it's worth asking the question, "Can this employee's value be increased if we make some minor changes in the environment in which he or she works?" For example, an employee who appears less able might benefit from more supervision or less. Look below the surface before making important decisions that affect people's lives.

> ## Work Backwards from Performance
>
> **Tricks of the Trade**
>
> When identifying factors that interfere with performance and discussing them during the performance review, start with performance and work backwards, looking in turn at behavior, system variables, and individual variables.

Advantages of Looking at Performance Broadly

Once you've committed to the broader view of performance outlined here and once you've explained it so your employees understand it, it profoundly changes the discussions and interactions in performance reviews. For example, rather than look at what the employee has done or not done in the past year (looking solely at behavior), you can look at the employee's contributions, then backtrack to behavior and individual variables. If this is done properly, it makes the employee far less defensive, since the beginning focus is on the company's goals and the work unit's goals.

In a business sense, this perspective is also much more useful. The cold, hard fact of business is that employees who do not contribute to the achievement of the company's goals become liabilities regardless of how they behave or their skills and abilities. Therefore, focusing on contribution makes the performance review process an important strategic business tool.

Finally, understanding performance in a broad sense opens the door to real problem solving that can be done *with* the employee. Since we no longer focus primarily on the employee's behavior but also look at the environment, that we are much more likely to identify barriers to performance we would never find if we focused only on the employee's individual characteristics. That makes the review process incredibly valuable as a business tool and relevant to managers and employees.

Manager's Checklist for Chapter 3

❏ Performance is best seen as the degree to which an employee contributes to the goals of the work unit and the goals of the organization.

❏ Performance (contribution) is determined by individual employee characteristics, system characteristics, and the interaction between the two. To improve performance, *all* of these need to be discussed and considered during the performance review.

❏ By considering system variables and what you and the company might do to improve an individual's perform-ance, you move the discussion toward a cooperative and non-defensive process.

❏ A person can be skilled, able, fast, and knowledgeable and still not be contributing or performing well, particularly if the system in which he or she works is faulty and presents significant barriers to performance. In these situations, focusing only on the person will not result in better per-formance.

❏ It's important that employees not be penalized by perform-ance problems that are beyond their control. A broad view of performance makes the review process more fair.

4

Documenting Performance and Rating and Ranking Systems

In most companies, managers are expected to complete forms or otherwise document what occurs during performance review meetings. We'll explain why this expectation exists. But before we get to that, let's discuss some issues about performance reviews and forms. Confusion about the use of forms is one of the major reasons why many performance reviews fail.

First, the forms you use should *not* be the focus of your performance review process. The forms serve a purpose, an important purpose, and that's to keep a record of the discussions that have taken place and any decisions or commitments made during the review process. However, they are *not* the reason why you do performance reviews.

Performance reviews are not about forms. They are about the communication between manager and employee for the purpose of looking at past performance, identifying ways to improve performance in the future, and planning for improvement.

Think about it like a marriage. Having a marriage certificate isn't the same as the "process of marriage." While the marriage certificate tells you a couple is officially married, it clearly doesn't mean the marriage is working or will endure. The marriage is a process that changes over time. The piece of paper isn't the marriage. The two people interacting in certain ways *is* the marriage.

It's the same with performance documentation. The performance review is a process. The documentation (much like the marriage certificate) may be useful, but it's not the review and by itself it's not likely to improve performance or work to anyone's benefit. Marriage certificates don't guarantee a good marriage. Forms don't guarantee a useful performance review or improve performance. People do.

> **Succeeding in Spite of Forms**
>
> Even if the review forms you're forced to use by your company are absolutely useless, it doesn't mean that performance reviews with your employees need to be useless too. When you concentrate on your discussion with the employee and work on solving problems to improve performance, the poor forms have less impact.

Second, most companies use the same form across a wide range of jobs. That means they are often so generic that their worth for any specific job is severely compromised.

Third, it's an unfortunate fact that the forms provided by companies for managers to use to document performance are often extremely flawed. If you focus on the completion of flawed forms, you are going to have extremely flawed reviews that have limited value.

Fourth, there's no perfect way to document performance or, for that matter, to evaluate performance. Each method has strengths and weaknesses. So, regardless of the forms given to you, you have to learn to work with them and sometimes to work around them, in order to make the most out of performance reviews. If you look at the performance review as a communications process, you'll be able to do that. If you look at performance reviews as filling out forms, it's going to be a wasted paper chase.

So What's the Point of Documentation?

Since there's no such thing as a perfect form or a perfect way of documenting performance, and since most methods and forms are severely flawed, you might be wondering why the documentation process is done at all. Why complete flawed forms? If the important part of the review is communication between manager and employee, maybe we could just ditch the forms.

In a simple and ideal world, maybe that would be best. Unfortunately, we don't live in that simple world and there are some good reasons why you are asked to complete forms to document performance.

Compelling Reason—Legal Issues

Over the last decades more and more employees have been taking employers to court over employment issues. Sometimes those lawsuits are justified; sometimes they're not. But one thing is sure: you want to protect yourself and your company from unwarranted or malicious lawsuits that have no basis in fact.

There are several areas of concern here. The first is the possibility that an employee will claim he or she has been punished and/or fired unlawfully or without reason. Laws on this issue vary from state to state and country to country. It may be you work in a location where the employer has the right to terminate employment for any reason or for no reason at all. If it's the latter, then there's really no threat on this point. However, if the law requires a solid reason, there's definitely a danger.

The second area of concern, perhaps more relevant to those of us in North America, is that an employee can claim that he or she has been punished, fired, or denied a promotion based on some illegal criterion. A person who is classified as part of a protected class might claim that being fired was a result of whatever factor entitles him or her to special protection. These claims fall under equal opportunity laws, which of course also vary from location to location. In the United States though, equal opportunity laws are federal, so if you are in the U.S. these laws apply to you and your employees can file complaints under those laws. In addition, your state may have laws that provide further protection of employees.

<table>
<tr><td>

TRICKS OF THE TRADE

A Signature Worth Its Weight

It's not enough to have documentation in the event of a discrimination lawsuit. You must demonstrate that the employee has received notice of any performance problems prior to dismissal. It's standard procedure for any documentation to be dated and signed by both parties. The signatures constitute an acknowledgment that the information has been shared, not necessarily an agreement on the content.
</td></tr>
</table>

So where does the documentation fit? If a complaint is filed that alleges some form of discrimination, you will need to show that the decision (promotion, demotion, firing) was made on the basis of legitimate performance issues. To do that, there must be some form of paper trail or documentation of performance difficulties, which shows three things:

- There have been problems.
- Those problems have been communicated to the employee.
- The employee has had a chance to address those problems.

In the absence of proper documentation, the court or legal authority is likely to determine that the decision had some illegal basis. In other words, once a complaint is filed, it is your company's responsibility to demonstrate it is false. The documentation is your offer of proof.

So, if you are wondering why human resources departments are so insistent on the completion of all of the relevant forms and other documentation, that's probably the explanation.

Other Reasons

Managers and organizations regularly make decisions about personnel. Here are a few questions that crop up regularly, almost every day:

| | Imperfections Galore **⚠ CAUTION! ⚠** |

Imperfections Galore

While performance reviews and documentation are used to make important decisions, you should always remember that the information is going to be faulty in some degree or other. Do not pretend that appraisal documents are objective assessments. Keep in mind that any records for any specific employee might be inaccurate.

- Who gets a raise?
- Who is to be laid off in tough times?
- Who needs to be moved to another job?
- Who is to be terminated due to poor performance?
- Who has potential and would benefit from development opportunities and training?

Apart from the legal issues mentioned earlier, it is in the interest of the company and the managers to make the best possible decisions. When times are tough, you want to lay off the least capable performers and not the best. You don't want to lose your best performers because you failed to recognize their contributions. You don't want to promote an employee who might have demonstrated performance problems three or four years ago. In other words you want to make the best decisions because when you make poor ones, you and the company suffer—and poor decisions reflect on *your* ability and your performance.

These decisions need to be made on some basis, on some data, if you prefer that term. You don't lay off specific people because you are in a bad mood or they happen to have annoyed you yesterday. You lay off people based on their records. It's the same for good performance. You promote, recognize, reward, and raise pay based on records.

Documentation is a means to track performance over time, so that data can be used to make decisions in the future. Even if that documentation is flawed, it's probably better than nothing. So, in that sense it's important.

Documentation Methods

Over the years a number of methods have developed and evolved for reviewing and documenting performance. In part that's been a result of recognizing that as of yet there's no perfect way to review and document performance. The more you know about the various approaches to documenting, the more able you'll be to make the best use of whatever system you are required to use or, if you have the option, to choose the system that makes the most sense to you. In the rest of this chapter, we're going to look at two formats—rating and ranking. We'll discuss the weaknesses of these two approaches and ways to maximize their effectiveness. In the next chapter, we'll cover other methods you may find useful, even preferable to rating and ranking.

Rating Systems

If you were to do a survey, you'd find that the most common method of recording or documenting performance is the rating system. You're probably familiar with ratings both as an employee and a manager. Typically the manager uses (sometimes is forced to use) a form that has a number of statements on it describing some or all of the following:

- job performance
- attitudes
- abilities
- skills
- behavior
- knowledge

For each statement, the manager is expected to rate the employee on a scale. The scales vary somewhat. Some have verbal descriptions for each point on the scale, such as "excellent," "average," and "needs improvement." Some have numeric systems running from one to three or one to five or even one to seven. Some use both numbers and a verbal descriptor for each point on the scale.

Examples of Scales

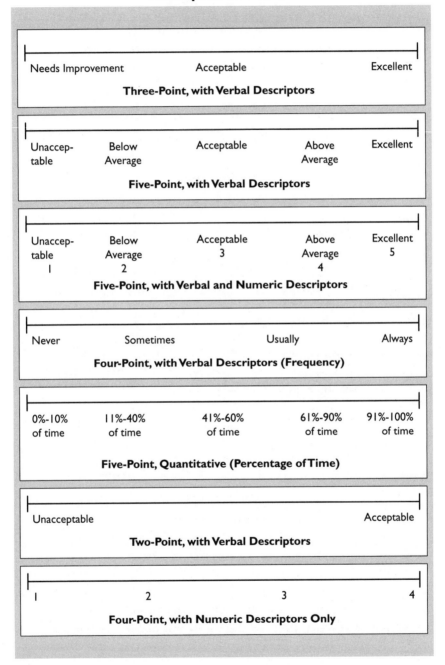

| Needs Improvement | Acceptable | Excellent |

Three-Point, with Verbal Descriptors

| Unaccep-table | Below Average | Acceptable | Above Average | Excellent |

Five-Point, with Verbal Descriptors

| Unaccep-table 1 | Below Average 2 | Acceptable 3 | Above Average 4 | Excellent 5 |

Five-Point, with Verbal and Numeric Descriptors

| Never | Sometimes | Usually | Always |

Four-Point, with Verbal Descriptors (Frequency)

| 0%-10% of time | 11%-40% of time | 41%-60% of time | 61%-90% of time | 91%-100% of time |

Five-Point, Quantitative (Percentage of Time)

| Unacceptable | Acceptable |

Two-Point, with Verbal Descriptors

| 1 | 2 | 3 | 4 |

Four-Point, with Numeric Descriptors Only

The quality and usefulness of these forms runs from absolutely atrocious to fair. It all depends on the skills of the form designer in writing the performance items so they are specific enough and clear enough to have meaning so a manager can use the scaled items intelligently. Let's look at two examples.

Is enthusiastic and motivated

Needs Improvement	2	3	4	Excellent
				5

This is an absolutely terrible example of a rating item: the item is not only useless, but bound to make even the most reasonable employee defensive and angry. The item is so vague that it's unlikely you could get any two people to agree on its meaning and it's likely that two people rating the same person would rate him or her quite differently. The rating given on such a vague item is as much a reflection on the rater/manager as on the employee.

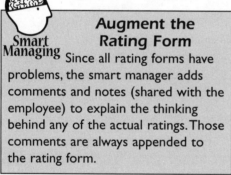

Smart Managing

Augment the Rating Form

Since all rating forms have problems, the smart manager adds comments and notes (shared with the employee) to explain the thinking behind any of the actual ratings. Those comments are always appended to the rating form.

Here's the real crunch, though. If the goal is to identify barriers to performance and improve performance, how does this item get us there? Clearly it doesn't, at least not on its own.

Now, let's look at another example.

Responds to customer requests within 24 hours

Almost Never	2	3	4	Everytime
				5

What differences can you identify between the two examples? The first thing that should jump out at you is that this example is far more specific and observable than the first one. If

one wanted, one could actually collect data to support an accurate rating. If you were to take two people and ask them what
this item means, you'd find they both understand its meaning in
the same way. Finally, it describes *behavior*, something the
employee actually does. This kind of item is far less likely to
push the employee into defensive behavior during the review
meeting, since it's not a comment on his or her personality and
is less personal than the first example.

The point here is that a form that has items like the second
example can be useful as a starting point for performance
improvement. If it turns out the employee hasn't been responding quickly enough to customer requests, then the next step is
clear: manager and employee can then discuss why that's happening. That's a much better, easier, and more comfortable discussion than would occur with our first example.

The first example is a starting point for arguments and bad
feelings. If you rate an employee as below average on "enthusi-
asm and motivation," where in heck do you go after that? How
can you address such a vague, nebulous description so
improvement happens? You can't.

Unfortunately, you may not be in a position to determine
which forms you use. You may have no choice, even if the forms
are truly terrible. We'll help you maximize the usefulness of these
forms in a moment. Before we turn to that topic, let's quickly
explain how these forms can be used and their limitations.

Their Value

Why are these forms so popular when they are often damaging
or ineffective? The answer is simple. They require little thought
to complete. For people who view the performance review as a
necessary evil and for people who just want to get it out of the
way, it seems perfect. Circle a few numbers on a scale, file it,
and be done with it. Even though such superficial usage is likely to cause real damage, the whole process can be completed
quickly. The rating forms also feel right—unless you think
about them.

Can rating forms be used for some good purpose? Yes. In the hands of a skilled manager and communicator, the forms can be used as a basic starting point for cooperative discussions of performance with employees. The forms can be used as a kind of shorthand that reflects the discussions that take place. That's a good thing, since it's likely you will be required to use these things at some point in your managerial career. Along with some basic written notes, the rating form can be used as documentation in the event of legal action.

Their Weaknesses

Even when you use the form intelligently, chances are it's not going to be specific enough to allow you to evaluate or review performance properly. Overemphasis on poorly designed forms damages the relationships between manager and employee. When numeric scales are used, there is an illusion of objectivity, because we associate numbers with data, but it's an illusion. There's a tendency to add up ratings on a form to give an overall performance number, but that resulting number, although it appears to have meaning, is absolutely meaningless and useless. Adding up individual ratings to come up with a single overall rating is like adding up the numbers on the jerseys of football players to decide which team is "better."

Maximizing Success

Does understanding that the rating approach is usually seriously flawed somehow help you to do a better job if you are forced to use such a system? Actually it does.

The danger in using any tool that has flaws is in assuming, believing, or hoping the tool is sound. For example, using a hammer that has a loose head isn't ideal, but if it's the only hammer available, you can make do, provided you know the head may fly off at any time and you use it carefully. It's the same with any performance appraisal method—and particularly with rating methods.

Since the real action and the real benefits come from the

communication and problem solving between manager and employee, a poor form need not mean failure. Here are a few suggestions.

- During the performance review, explain to the employee that, although you're required to complete the form, the actual ratings are less important than the discussion and less important than any other written comments append-ed to the form.
- You *must* augment the ratings with written comments that explain the ratings you're giving the employee. Scale numbers are meaningless without explanations, both to the employee and for future decisions. Some forms have space for comments on each item. If your forms have space, use it. If not, append additional notes so they're a permanent part of the record. This also gives you addi-tional legal protection.
- Tell the employee that he or she can and should make any written comments that you will gladly add to the record and the rating form. That reassures the person that he or she won't be harmed by a set of numbers with-out a context.
- Don't play God. You and the employee should discuss the ratings. You might even negotiate. The two of you don't have to agree, just to better understand.
- In the performance review meeting, the discussion of the appropriate rating should take only a small percentage of the total meeting time.

Ranking Systems

While the rating system is designed to evaluate an employee along some imaginary scale, a ranking system is intended to evaluate an employee by comparing him or her with all of the other employees in similar positions within a company. The result is some indication of where the employee lies, in percent-age terms, relative to his or her peers.

Depending on the form, an employee could be ranked as last in the company or first in the company or in terms of percentiles, e.g., a percentile of 55 means the employee is "better" than 55% of his or her peers.

On what basis is the comparison made? That basis varies widely.

Sometimes, in its worst form, a ranking system is based on adding together the numbers from rating form items and giving an overall "performance number," which then serves as the basis for ranking the employee.

The comparison may also be made on the basis of an observable and quantifiable number, such as sales per quarter or new clients signed up. Although rankings can be somewhat justified with simple things like sales numbers, there are a lot of problems associated with the process.

Their Value

Ranking systems have become a bit more common due to their use and endorsement by former General Electric CEO, Jack Welch, who suggested ranking employees each year and then firing the bottom 10%. There may be no arguing with his success at GE, but there's considerable doubt that the use of a ranking system was the key to his success.

You have to go a ways to identify what ranking systems actually contribute. One argument is that it places employees in similar jobs in direct competition with each other; the theory is that this competition (sometimes rather cutthroat) will improve the performance of all involved. That's a possibility. But the disadvantages of such a system (outlined below) are almost always going to outweigh any performance improvements gained this way.

In almost all situations, ranking employees is a poor idea. However, if it can work anywhere, it's most likely to be where the following conditions exist:

- There are objective and measurable criteria on which to base rankings (e.g., money earned, customers recruited).

- Nothing else is expected of the employees than to perform according to the specific, narrow criteria you use (e.g., make more money or recruit more customers).
- You have no desire to have your employees work together and help each other.
- You want a cutthroat work environment *inside* your company.

Their Weaknesses

Ranking systems are only as good as the validity of the criteria you use to compare employees. For example, tallying up the ratings and then ranking employees based on the sum of their ratings is mathematically unjustified and unfair. Rating systems simply aren't precise enough.

If you use simple and specific criteria like money earned, that's a bit better, but this doesn't work if you're concerned with other employee behaviors. For example, your top-ranked salesperson may make his money by cheating, sabotaging his coworkers, hiding resources, or otherwise impeding the success of his colleagues/competitors. That works if your performance objective is to have a top-ranked salesperson— but not if you want to improve *overall* sales levels across all salespeople. Your top-ranked salesperson may actually be costing you money due to his negative effect on those around him.

Ranking systems not only might not help you achieve your objectives, but also can create unhealthy competition among the people you need to work together. Using a ranking system tied to salary increases is the best way to create bad feelings, arguments, and even more nasty problems in the workplace.

Let's return to the issue of improving performance. Ranking systems do not provide enough information about employee performance to help employees identify what they have to do to improve. It's that simple. A numeric ranking only tells an employee where he or she stands in relation to other employees. It provides no information about getting better.

> **⚠ CAUTION!**
>
> ### Nobody Thinks They Are Average
>
> If you have to use the term "average" to describe an employee (either in rating or in ranking), be aware that research tells us that 80% of workers in various fields actually see themselves as above average. That's statistically impossible, of course, but that perception means you're bound to insult a significant number of employees if you label their performance as "average."

It's true that you can augment the ranking system with a process that tries to identify why the employee ranks below average. Unfortunately, however, there's a problem here. In a ranking system, by definition, there must always be a significant number of people who are "below average."

That's the fatal flaw with all ranking systems. A ranking system implies that there must always be people who are below average, average, above average, and so on. You can't have 10 people who are the best in terms of sales, right? You can have only one.

This isn't a problem if you have a broad range of skills and abilities in your workplace and a wide spread of performance. However, that's not always the case. In fact, if your hiring practices are good, all your employees should be skilled. The differences among them will be less than you'd find if you chose 50 people off the street at random.

So here's the problem. What if you have employees who are all excellent and differ little in terms of productivity? The ranking system is still going to require you to label some as "best," some as "average," and some as "below average" or worse. That's nuts. Even worse, if you decide to terminate the bottom 10% of your ranked staff, it's not likely the replacements will be better, if the bottom 10% that you let go are better than the average in other companies or in the job market.

Maximizing Success

I don't think you can maximize success with employee ranking systems. Your best-case scenario is to try to minimize the damage such a system causes.

If you are stuck with one, then here is my counsel. Try to get something different to use. Lobby other managers, human resources personnel, and anybody you can grab and convince that a ranking system is both unfair and mathematically flawed and that it creates hopelessly destructive conflict in the workplace.

Make it clear to your employees that, although they may be ranked and paid according to their rankings, you expect that they will help each other and certainly not do anything to interfere with the success of others. Monitor the situation carefully.

Manager's Checklist for Chapter 4

❏ There is no method of documenting or evaluating performance that is flawless. Your job is to understand the flaws and work around the weaknesses of the system you're using.

❏ The forms are not the review. The value of the review is in the discussion between employee and manager and not in the circling of numbers on forms. If you remember that, you can do well with any documentation system, no matter how flawed.

❏ Documentation is necessary to protect you and the company from unjustified accusations of illegal or discriminatory labor practices.

❏ Documentation, when properly done, is also often used as a basis to make personnel decisions. The better the basis for the documentation, the better the decisions.

❏ Augment both rating and ranking systems with written comments, which should reflect your discussions with the employee.

Documenting Performance—
Narrative, Critical Incident, MBO, 360-Degree Feedback, and Other Methods

The most common system used to document performance involves rating employees. Other methods can be more useful, however, if your goal is to improve performance and work in partnership with your employees. In this chapter we'll discuss some of these other methods—narratives, the critical incident method, standards-based/management by objectives, and one of the more recent innovations, 360-degree feedback. As you go through these methods, keep in mind that there are variations within each method. If you want more information about any specific method, consider some of the books listed in the bibliography at the back of the book.

Narrative

The narrative method of documenting and reviewing performance involves "writing a story" to describe the performance of an employee. The best way to clarify this method is to show you an example of a simple, short narrative. The following is a narrative written for receptionist and switchboard operator Clarence.

Clarence works well under pressure and handles phone calls efficiently and effectively. His ability to stay on top of both calls and in-person visitors is a bonus, and several clients have commented on how polite and helpful he is. On occasion Clarence has misdirected calls, resulting in a few customers feeling they've gotten the runaround. This is probably due to not having had the roles of staff properly explained to him.

Clarence has shown the ability to learn new skills and a desire to take on additional responsibilities.

I consider Clarence a valuable employee and someone who might train to do more advanced tasks to be considered for promotion.

In this very short example, Clarence's major job responsibilities are covered, with comments about each. Narratives need not be limited to descriptions of job behavior or abilities, but can also include plans for training and promotion and results of problem diagnostics and performance problem solving.

The narrative method is exceedingly flexible. A narrative can be about almost anything and can be written on a supplied form, typed into a computer, or just written longhand. It can be composed of one single general narrative or it can be structured using pre-designated categories. For example, a narrative form might include categories like "Punctuality and Attendance," "Interaction with Customers," and "Sales Success" or use any categories relevant to a particular employee's work. The narrative can be structured in almost any way, with many categories or very few.

Narratives can also include some basic rating elements, so the information recorded can be summarized. It's not uncommon for a narrative to contain an overall summary section, which requires the narrator to indicate whether the person's overall performance is in need of improvement, satisfactory, or excellent. Those ratings, however, are not the focus of the process. The narrative is the focus.

You can use various methods for coming up with the final narrative for an employee.

The worst way to do it is to sit in your office, write the narrative, and then stick it in front of the employee at the review meeting for his or her signature. That completely misses the point, which is for you and the employee to work together to identify and solve problems.

A more productive way is for you and the employee to prepare for the review meeting by making notes and jotting down phrases that describe the employee's performance. Those notes become the basis for the review discussion. During that discussion, you work with the employee to draft a narrative that both of you feel is accurate, fair, and useful for both of you.

A third way is to have two review meetings. At the first, you and the employee discuss performance and make notes. Next, one of you writes the narrative. Then, you meet again, let's say a week later, to discuss the narrative.

> **TRICKS OF THE TRADE**
>
> **Time to Think**
> Before finalizing narrative-based review documents, it's best to allow time to think about the content before signing off on it. Once a preliminary narrative has been drafted, both you and the employee should have a few days to think about it and suggest modifications before everything is finalized.

Strengths

The power of the narrative lies in its extreme flexibility. This allows managers to customize the contents of the review according to context, type of job, length of employment, or other factors that seem appropriate. That means that the same method of evaluation can be used for the CEO and for the maintenance staff. What would differ would be the categories and content, which would derive from the major job responsibilities of each. For example, one of the categories on a maintenance staff review might be "Knowledge of Cleaning Substances and Methods." Clearly this category wouldn't be used with a CEO, but "Knowledge of Accounting and Standard Financial Practices" might be.

This permits the narratives to be extremely job-specific, which makes them more helpful in improving performance. Contrast this with the standard use of ratings, which, if used across job types, tend to use much too general review or evaluative dimensions. If you are required to use a ratings format, the narrative can also be used to add specificity to the ratings. In that combination, you'd explain each rating with a short comment or narrative.

Another advantage of the narrative is that it doesn't create an illusion of objectivity, as is often the case with rating systems. It is what it appears to be.

Weaknesses

Narratives share a common weakness with any review methods that rely on an "end of year" process. They are based on both parties' abilities to remember what's happened over an entire year and to summarize a year's events some time after the facts. The solution, of course, is obvious: to have regular performance reviews during the year, perhaps as often as once a month, where manager and employee can discuss performance and take notes. These "interim" meetings can be as short as five minutes, if they are done efficiently.

Narratives also rely on the skills of the narrator. It's not easy to write a clear, concise description of an employee's accomplishments, abilities, successes, and possible performance deficits. It's not easy at all. The price of flexibility is that managers need to do much more during the review process than, for example, if they were using a rating system, where all they have to do is circle a few numbers. Then again, if that's all that's done—circling a few numbers—the benefits of the review drop to zero.

Some people feel that narratives are not useful because they don't yield an easy way to classify employees using some kind of overall assessment of performance. People like numbers. There's some odd comfort in being able to sum up Jeff's performance as

MISTAKE PROOFING

Using Shorter Notes Instead

A performance review narrative doesn't have to be a story. If you don't feel comfortable with your ability to write prose, you may find that writing the review as notes or as points works better for you. Provided what you write is clear and understandable, there's no problem doing a narrative that isn't really a "story."

a "68" and Jane's performance as an "82." The ability to summarize a year's performance in one number is not part of the narrative method. This may be a plus, though, since those kinds of summaries are often inaccurate, still subjective, and likely to create friction between employee and manager.

Overall, though, the flexibility of narratives is exceedingly useful and outweighs the perceived weaknesses. However, if managers and employees lack the ability to write clearly and concisely, the narrative method may not be effective.

Maximizing Success

As with other methods, it's important that managers and employees undergo some training in the use of the narrative. Since writing narratives is more demanding than more structured approaches, it's probably even more important that managers have the chance to practice writing them in a classroom setting where they can receive feedback.

It's important not to rely completely on memory and, for this reason, the manager should note information about each employee's performance throughout the year, preferably as part of the ongoing communication process we've discussed elsewhere.

A well-designed narrative recording form can be extremely useful. The ideal form provides enough structure and categories to guide manager and employee, but also allows customization of categories or comments to fit the employee's job.

Again, as with all of the other review methods we've described, focus on the process and the discussion and don't overemphasize what is recorded on paper. If you keep in mind that performance improves as a result of the *discussions* and not because of the writing and recording, you'll be in good shape with this review tool.

Critical Incident

The critical incident method of reviewing or documenting performance

Not Just the Negatives

Avoid the tendency to focus narratives on things that have gone wrong. Believe it or not, even with under-performing employees, it's likely they are doing more things right than wrong. This should be reflected in the narratives. There's no need to gloss over problems, but just don't forget the positives.

involves recording instances of important events (incidents) where the employee has performed well or performed less effectively. Both employee behavior (e.g., yelled at customer) and results (e.g., customer cancelled order) can be included in the "incidents net." To keep the recording process from becoming chaotic, you can use forms or other methods that provide categories. For example, a recording form might include categories like "customer relations," "punctuality," or "teamwork."

The recording of critical incidents is normally done in a narrative form, but it tends to be more focused since it's driven by observations of specific events and not general impressions, as is usually the case with the straight narrative.

It's possible to use this method in several ways. The manager can be responsible for documenting critical incidents, particularly when he or she is in a position to regularly observe employee performance. In a call center, where the manager may periodically monitor how calls are handled, the critical incident method works well. Where the manager is not able to monitor performance directly, it's pos-

Specific Wording

Here's a partial example of wording you might use as *part* of a critical incident report. Note how specific it is. "Sept. 17: Observed John repeatedly interupting other staff at team meeting, rolling eyes, sighing, with general body language suggesting anger and frustration. Staff members indicated this was upsetting."

sible to use a less conventional method. The employee can document successes and problems as they occur. A good example of the critical incident process is when a police officer documents the facts of a case, such as the apprehension of a suspect. That document can be used later for discussion with a superior to analyze what went well and what, if anything, could have gone better.

Strengths

The critical incident method is most appropriate and effective when the manager directly observes and supervises the employees regularly, so he or she can monitor important events. It is less a way to record performance on a yearly basis and much better suited to a situation where manager and employee are speaking about performance on a very regular basis.

If we compare the pure narrative with the critical incident method, the one advantage of the critical incident method, when it's done properly, is that it involves recording specific observable situations, while narratives tend to be more general. The more specific the information you make available to employees, the more likely the employees will be able to use that information to improve their performance.

Weaknesses

Unless there is regular monitoring and paperwork is kept up to date, this method is more suited to ongoing performance communication than for use in a once-a-year performance review meeting. Keep in mind that many jobs do not lend themselves to direct observation of events and that employees may feel "over-monitored" and mistrusted if managerial observation occurs often.

Maximizing Success

Recording of critical incidents should be descriptive and not evaluative. That is, you record what you hear or see and not your opinion about what happened. Think of it like writing a news story—it's who, what, when, where, and perhaps why. The place for evaluating or appraising the value of what you see is in face-to-face discussions with the employee. Ideally you present what you saw and encourage the employee to evaluate his or her behavior and diagnose the problem.

There's a tendency to record only negative incidents. Be alert to the positive events and situations where the employee has performed well.

Standards-Based or Management by Objectives

You may have come across the term management by objectives (MBO). MBO refers to a process for managing performance, which includes the performance review as only one part. This may sound familiar since, in Chapter 2, we explained the relationship between a performance review and performance management.

MBO is a bit different from performance management. The MBO system focuses on whether employees have "hit the target," where the target is outlined in objectives and performance standards—descriptions of desired job performance. Performance management, as we described it in Chapter 2, does not require objectives and standards.

Sometimes those objectives are also called performance *standards*. So we don't confuse you,

> **Standards (performance)** A set of expectations, applicable to a specific employee, outlining what the employee is expected to achieve. Ideally standards of performance are measurable in an objective way and focus on observable behavior or results.

we're going to talk about standards-based performance reviews, rather than the bigger MBO system.

On the surface, standards-based performance reviews are simple. At some point the employee and the manager set standards of performance to describe what the employee should accomplish and how well the employee should perform. At the performance *review* meeting, the discussion centers on whether the employee has hit those goals. In the simplest form of standards-based performance reviews, the standards are set at the beginning of a year and the review meeting is held a year later. Of course the effectiveness of this approach relies on the communication, diagnosis and problem solving that goes on year-round.

What does a standard look like? Extensive guidelines exist to help managers and employees write standards so they work well, but here are a few basics. Standards need to be measurable and measurement should be as objective as possible. The standards written for any particular employee should cover the major job tasks—the most important things an employee must achieve—and they should focus on the results the employee is supposed to create. Here are a few examples that might apply to a customer service representative:

- Replies to all customer inquiries within one working day
- Receives a customer rating of at least four on a five-point scale
- Has no more than 5% of customers call back for clarification

Notice how specific these standards are. Each of these can be measured objectively and even precisely. For comparison, here are some poorly written standards, again applicable to a customer service representative:

- Is polite to all customers
- Receives few customer complaints
- Solves problems quickly

These are *not* measurable because they are far too vague and are not based on clear criteria. The differences between the first set and the second set may seem unimportant, but when you get to the performance review discussion, you'll find that standards expressed like those in the second set are real fire-starters. The more vague the standards, the more likely the employee and the manager won't be able to come to agreement on whether the employee has achieved the standards.

In a standards-based system, the review meeting focuses on manager and employee coming to that kind of agreement. However, again, we

Documenting Results TRICKS OF THE TRADE
Standards that are properly written are relatively simple to document. Either an employee has "hit the mark" or not. Generally the documentation of the achievement of standards can be reduced to a simple Achieved/Did Not Achieve dichotomy. Sometimes a third category, "exceeded the standard," is also included.

emphasize that the power and effectiveness of a standards-based approach lies with the discussions that occur about why standards were achieved and why they were not and from planning to remove barriers that occurred so they will not impede performance in the future.

Strengths

Standards-based or management-by-objectives approaches have a number of advantages over many of the other methods. Perhaps the most compelling is that a standards-based approach encourages face-to-face communication between manager and employee to identify the degree to which the employee has achieved the standards or objectives. On balance, with a standards-based approach, the employee is more likely to receive information detailed enough to improve performance—*provided* that the process is done properly.

The system is flexible, since employees can have different standards of performance, even if their job descrip-

Job- or Employee-Based Standards Smart Managing
Some believe that all employees doing identical jobs should have the same performance standards. Another way to look at it is employees can contribute to the company in different ways, even if they have the same job descriptions, so it makes sense to base standards on what each employee really does, and not the job description. Use what's best for your situation, but err on the side of flexibility.

tions are similar. Unlike rating systems used across job positions, the standards are completely customizable; in fact, they must be customized.

The system is particularly useful and relatively easy to apply to job tasks that can be measured relatively easily and objectively. It can still be used for complex jobs, but it takes more skill on the part of the manager to use it effectively.

It should be clear by now that the performance standards method involves a lot of upfront work, but less work at the performance review. The result of the extensive work in setting standards (planning performance) is that the employee should leave the standard-setting meeting with a very clear understanding of what he or she is to accomplish during the upcoming period. Not only is that understanding likely in itself to improve performance, but it promotes self-evaluation throughout the year. Employees who know where they need to go are generally able to assess, on their own and throughout the year, whether they are getting there.

Weaknesses

It is extremely hard to write performance standards that are both meaningful and objectively measurable. There's a saying that goes like this: "It's easy to measure trivial things, but it's very hard to measure important things meaningfully." It applies here. For practical reasons, you can't have hundreds of standards that apply to an employee's performance. Perhaps 10 to 20 is the maximum—and even that's a lot. Identifying which standards to use and writing them in objective ways is an art form and generally requires training for those involved in writing standards. That may mean training both managers and employees.

Some managers complain that the standard-setting process is too time-consuming and difficult. There's no question that the upfront work involved with this system is much more demanding than, let's say, for a narrative or rating system, where the upfront work can be almost zero. That may appear as a weakness, but it's more of a shifting of the work from the performance-review phase to the performance-planning phase.

Maximizing Success

How can you get the most benefit from a standards-based system? Recognize the following facts:

- Objectives and standards set with the employee are not going to represent the entire universe of things the employee does or all the ways the employee contributes.
- Objectives and standards and the process of determining if they have been met appear to eliminate subjectivity and opinions. That is not always the case, even for those who are very skilled at writing standards.
- As with any performance review system, the point is not to catch someone doing something wrong or to punish, but to set up the conditions by which performance can be improved and help the employee monitor himself or herself.

Since it's so hard to write standards well, here's an important tip. It's less important to write "perfect" standards than it is that both employee and manager understand what is expected of the employee. Standards are tools for communication. That's why it's so important that standards be written either by the employee or by the employee and the manager in collaboration. Once you and the employee understand the expectations in the same way, the process of review is easy. In other words, the importance of setting standards lies with the discussion of them. There's a point at which it becomes counterproductive to try to get each standard "perfect."

360-Degree Feedback

The 360-degree feedback approach for documenting and reviewing performance is the newest entry on the scene. In the 1990s it emerged as a method for reviewing and improving the performance of managers. It has been extended and used with employees at all levels.

360-degree feedback
The process of gathering information about job performance from multiple perspectives to provide a more complete view of that performance. Because 360 usually relies on ratings, it's also called *multi-rater evaluation*.

The 360-degree feedback process involves collecting information about performance from multiple sources or multiple raters. For example, a review of a manager's performance might involve collecting data, opinions, and observations from his or her employees, immediate supervisor, colleagues, and even customers. A review of an employee without supervisory responsibilities might entail eliciting the perceptions of his or her supervisor, customers, and colleagues. Typically those perceptions are collected using a rating system, so in a sense 360-degree feedback is a subset of the ratings method, with all the advantages and drawbacks of any rating system.

The theory makes sense. If you want to improve performance, you can learn more by taking into account the perspectives of a number of "involved parties," rather than only the perspective of the employee's immediate supervisor. The implementation, however, is problematic.

Clouding the issue considerably is that the sale of 360-degree feedback instruments, particularly computer-based tools to make the process easier, has become a huge and very lucrative business. Because of the amount of money involved in the industry, there's a huge level of hyperbole and a lot of exaggerated success stories out there. The 360 method has become one of the more common "management fads." That's not to say it can't be useful, but often the problems associated with it are ignored in favor of an unbalanced focus on its strengths.

Strengths

In a well-functioning work environment where there's a high level of trust, the tool has value if it's implemented properly. In situations where the recipient of the feedback does not trust the people who provide it, the tendency is for the recipient to discount the feedback, attribute negative feedback to ulterior motives, and feel angry or even attacked. However, where workplace trust is high, so that people provide feedback in the true spirit of performance improvement and recipients take the ratings and comments at face value, the 360 method can be very useful.

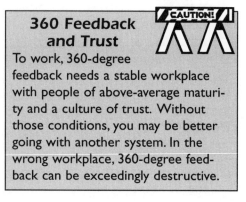

360 Feedback and Trust

To work, 360-degree feedback needs a stable workplace with people of above-average maturity and a culture of trust. Without those conditions, you may be better going with another system. In the wrong workplace, 360-degree feedback can be exceedingly destructive.

Apart from expanding the scope of feedback available for performance improvement, there's another positive effect of the 360-degree method. It reminds people that it's important to pay attention to the effects their actions have on people other than the boss or the customer.

For example, it's possible a salesperson might excel at sales by competing in a destructive way with the other salespeople at the firm. While this person's sales figures may look great, his or her actions may be hurting the sales of colleagues. Feedback collected from coworkers reminds the employee that he or she is not only responsible for selling, but also expected to contribute to the success of the other salespeople—or at least not interfere with their success.

This example also illustrates that a 360-feedback system can provide information that we would normally not have to improve performance. A performance review system led by a manager would likely miss the effect of the salesperson's actions on others' sales, particularly if the manager focused on sales numbers.

Weaknesses

The first question we need to ask of any review method is whether it's likely to improve performance. There are two very important weaknesses with the 360-degree feedback approach

MISTAKE PROOFING

Assessing Readiness

How do you know whether 360 feedback will work in your workplace? A manager's perceptions of trust in the workplace are often dead wrong. Whether you are thinking of implementing 360 feedback or you use it currently, it's very important that you elicit information from your employees about their feelings and reactions to it. Don't discount those feelings in your decision making.

in that respect. The first is the insistence by most "360 experts" that feedback be anonymous. The idea, of course, is that protecting the identity of feedback providers will make them more comfortable conveying their opinions, since they need not fear reprisal from the recipient. There's some merit in that. Let's assume that it's true, although it's by no means a proven conclusion. How does anonymity affect the value of the feedback and the chances that performance can be improved by that feedback?

Before we answer that question, let's review a fundamental weakness of any rating-based system, since 360 feedback is almost always rating-based. The information contained in a rating, whether it's a number or a verbal descriptor, is exceedingly limited. How does a rating of "two on a scale of five" or "four out of seven" help an employee do his or her job better? By itself it doesn't.

When the recipient can discuss the rating and the reasons behind it, then there's a possibility of improving performance. In fact, whatever value there is to rating systems comes from the discussions between rater and recipient. When the person giving the rating or the feedback is anonymous, the recipient can't ask for additional clarification or information. In an anonymous system, the mechanism for performance improvement is lost.

There's a second problem with anonymity. People almost always take into account the source of the feedback when deciding on its validity and value. As an example, when you receive feedback from your children, your spouse, your boss, and a total stranger, there's no doubt that you treat the four comments differently, depending on the source. When feedback is anonymous, it creates psychological ambiguity: the recipient needs to know the source so he or she can evaluate the context and decide whether the feedback is credible. Otherwise, it's confusing, even annoying.

Maximizing Success

In accordance with the advice of most "experts," 360 feedback should never be used to make decisions about pay or rewards and punishments. There are some potential legal problems that occur if you use 360 results in this way, not to mention some serious issues of fairness and concerns about the objective accuracy of 360 feedback data.

I do not recommend the use of the 360 process as a stand-alone system, as a formal system that applies to all employees in the organization and is mandatory. There's a simple reason for this. We know that feedback not explicitly requested by the recipient is almost always seen as intrusive and imposed. The power of 360 is maximized when employees enter into the process voluntarily and where there is sufficient trust so employees feel they can volunteer to be a part of the process.

The 360 process is best applied informally. There is no reason why a manager can't consult his or her staff for feedback at any time. In fact, that's a great way of improving managerial performance. You don't need a mandatory system to do so. Likewise for employees. Employees who trust each other will naturally elicit opinions and feedback from their coworkers.

Finally, contrary to the opinions of most experts, I do not believe anonymous feedback without face-to-face discussion is useful, fair, or constructive. I also believe that if someone is going to offer feedback on another's performance, that person should be willing to put his or her name on the dotted line. That's not to say that identifying the sources of feedback eliminates problems. It's just that performance improves when the feedback contains enough information and where information can be *exchanged*. I've seen informal 360 methods yield excellent results in team contexts, although the results usually depend on having a skilled facilitator to keep the process on a positive path.

Use of Technological Tools

Over the last decade, a new trend in performance reviews has emerged—the use of technological tools to make performance reviews easier. In fact, the development of software for this purpose has become a major growth industry. While these technological tools are, in theory, designed to *assist* in the performance review process, they often actually *replace* the face-to-face performance review process. It's important to discuss these innovations, since their misuse can destroy the review process.

TRICKS OF THE TRADE

Tools Limit

When someone is given a tool for a performance review, there's a strong tendency to use that tool—and use it with the least possible effort. Technology-based tools tend to help people do the *minimum* required by those tools. In performance reviews, that doesn't work. Don't rely on the tool given you. Augment it to improve performance.

Let me tell you a true story, although without identifying the players. At a conference on performance management at which I was speaking, I happened to engage in conversation with a human resource specialist who was very excited about an amazing new technological application used to provide feedback to employees. Since I hadn't heard of this particular technological breakthrough, I asked a few questions. Here's the gist of the conversation.

> It's amazing. All the manager needs to do to give feedback to the employee is call up a phone number and enter in some codes and numbers. That way, nobody has to be in the same place and it's incredibly efficient. The manager calls this number, see, and touch-tone inputs the ID number of the employee he wishes to review. Then the computer reads off some rating scale items and asks the manager to rate the employee on a scale of one to five. We use one of those computer voices that sounds like a real person, so the

process doesn't seem cold or impersonal. The whole review process takes almost no time. Then, the responses collected this way are summarized and printed out and given to the employee. Also, we get a copy for our files; we can store it electronically so it cuts down on the paperwork. It's worked so well with manager feedback that we're going to set things up to get information about employees from coworkers too.

Since it's rare that anyone bothers to spend money to evaluate whether any particular performance review system actually works, this particular HR person focused on the apparent efficiency of the system. Yes, it was fast. Yes, it reduced paperwork. Yes, some managers, who preferred to have limited contact with their employees, loved it. On the surface, at least to some of the folks at this company, it was a success. But it sure gives the phrase "phoning it in" a new meaning.

By now you should realize the absolute folly of such a system where the technology has replaced real communication and interaction between people and where employees can't get detailed enough information from review and feedback systems to *improve* their performance. In this case, the technology has simply allowed managers to do a poor job more quickly and easily.

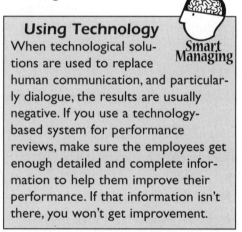

Using Technology

When technological solutions are used to replace human communication, and particularly dialogue, the results are usually negative. If you use a technology-based system for performance reviews, make sure the employees get enough detailed and complete information to help them improve their performance. If that information isn't there, you won't get improvement.

Smart Managing

That's sometimes the case with technology. It makes it easier to go to heck in a handbasket. We can now do really stupid things we shouldn't be doing at all, but more quickly. What we are doing may be absolutely pointless, but goodness, we can do it fast!

This example is an extreme. But computer-based review systems are becoming much more popular and, although they can be a boon, more often one finds that they are being badly misapplied.

Strengths

There's nothing wrong with using computers to help in the review process, to reduce paperwork and streamline some of the overhead of documenting and reviewing performance. Some of the simpler applications involve using a word processor to complete a narrative type review, using a master document template provided by HR. Something like that, when it isn't used to replace human communication, can save time. Rating systems can make use of computers, but unfortunately the computerization of these systems doesn't improve them. So if the initial paper-based rating system is poor, it's likely the computer-based one will end up even worse. The strengths of technology lie in its ability to record and store information—*not* in communicating information in ways that will support performance improvement.

Weaknesses

Since computers provide the illusion of efficiency, it's almost sure that the computer-based process is perceived as *replacing* the essential human parts of the review process. If and when that happens, the process becomes valueless for improving performance, and perhaps damaging.

Maximizing Success

Use computers and performance review software as tools for recording and storing information. Do *not* rely on them or the printouts they produce to communicate with employees about performance. As with paper forms, don't equate completing the computer-based process with the performance review.

Again, as with forms, you can use the collected information as a basis for beginning a discussion with the employee. The data should never be given to the employee without that discussion.

When the computer-based system uses ratings, keep in mind that the ratings themselves convey very little information to the employee and that it's important to append comments for the employee to use and in the interests of fairness. If the stored information is accessed at a later date, the reader can put the ratings into context.

Manager's Checklist for Chapter 5

❏ The common thread among all the review methods is that none of them will help improve performance without effective face-to-face communication. A good manager, with strong communication skills, can make any method work. A poor manager can't make any of them work.

❏ If the system your company forces you to use doesn't meet your needs, there's no reason you can't augment it with features from other methods. Don't let company dictates restrict you.

❏ Performance reviews are like car repairs: it's pay now ... or pay a lot more later. When the upfront work is done properly, the actual performance reviews become easy to complete. And if you don't do performance reviews at all, the long-term cost is huge.

❏ The methods we've described in these two chapters can be implemented in a number of ways. Some of them, in fact most of them, require in-depth understanding of the method in question. Consider doing additional reading on methods that interest you and, once you've chosen a specific method, consider training for yourself and your staff. Well-informed and skilled employees make the review process much easier.

❏ There is no perfect or magic method to reviewing and documenting performance. Understand that every method has flaws and it's up to you to work around those flaws.

Performance Planning—

The Answer to Almost Any Review Problem

Take a look at these very common questions:

- How can I reduce disagreements and bad feelings during the performance review?
- How can I get across the idea that the performance review is something the employee and I do together?
- How do I improve the fairness of the performance review process?
- I find it hard, and sometimes impossible, to measure performance objectively. How do I deal with this issue?
- We base pay and promotions on the results of the performance review. We all know our measurement process is subjective and seriously flawed. How do I deal with this problem?
- I find it difficult to sit in the "seat of power": I want my employees to move toward being able to evaluate themselves. What do I need to do to make that happen?
- How do I make sure that the job tasks the employee does are really contributing to the work unit?

You'd think that the answers to these and other very important questions about performance reviews lie in altering *how* the
performance review meeting is conducted. After all, if we are
talking about challenges related to performance reviews, doesn't
it make sense to look for solutions within the performance
review meeting? Well, no, it doesn't, because many of these
problems have roots elsewhere or can be solved only by focusing on other parts of the performance management system.

The answers to all of these questions, and many others, are
in doing your performance planning properly. By doing the
work upfront, you eliminate a lot of work and difficulties at the
back end. In this chapter you're going to learn more about what
performance planning involves, why it's so important, and how
to use it effectively.

What Is Performance Planning?

You may recall that Chapter 2 explained the links between
the larger performance management process and performance reviews. At that point we defined *performance planning*
as follows:

> Performance planning is the starting point for performance
> management and it is essential in laying the groundwork for
> effective reviews later on. Performance planning is the
> process of communication between manager and employee
> intended to create agreement about what the employee is to
> do, how well he or she needs to do it, and why, when, and
> how success is to be determined.

Analogy: Building a House

Perhaps the best way to understand the performance planning
process is to use an analogy, that of building a house. Except
for very simple dwellings, only a fool would build a house without a comprehensive set of plans for that house. There are a lot
of reasons for developing a set of house plans.

First, the process of working with an architect, let's say,
helps the house owner define and refine what he or she wants

from the house, what it should look like, what features it should have, and how it should function. This is apart from the actual value of the plans to guide construction. The thought process associated with planning is valuable in and of itself.

Process Is Important

Whether we talk about performance reviews, performance planning, or any other part of performance management, keep in mind that it's not just the outcomes that are important. Even if you didn't end up with an actual performance plan, the performance planning discussion is invaluable in and of itself.

Second, the plan helps to organize the resources needed to build the house. A good set of building plans will tell us whom we need to involve in the building process, because that may depend on what we want as part of the house. For example, if we're building a swimming pool, we need different amounts of physical material (e.g., concrete, piping) than if we were not putting in a pool. The pool might require that we arrange for "people resources" or contractors who specialize in building pools. Having the plan in advance allows us to allocate the resources needed to turn the plan into a house in a timely, organized way.

Third, the plan serves as a guide for construction. The complete set of plans can be used by the plumber, the electrician, the drywall contractor, and all the other players involved. It guides the construction process so that less direct supervision is required while the work is being done.

Fourth, the plan allows for coordination of work. Having the whole plan allows us an overview of the process, so the work can be organized and coordinated for maximum efficiency.

Fifth, the plan specifies what the final product is to look like and how it is to function. It sets out the standards to which the house is to be built. That makes evaluating the construction process much easier, both during construction and after the house is completed. Both are important. If your plan indicates the use of oak moldings and the carpenter is using cheaper hemlock, you'll be able to notice this discrepancy during early construction, with a simple walk-through, and insist the carpenter return to the original specifications as in the agreement. In other words, the plan helps you catch problems during the building process. We call the process of identifying early on when something is wrong *red flagging*.

The plan makes it easier for you to go back to the builders or contractors when and if they haven't met the specifications or standards. Did they use 2x4-inch joists instead of 2x6's as specified? You have recourse since the plan clearly stated the relevant requirements. The plan permits more unambiguous documentation of what was planned versus what was created.

> **Key Term**
>
> **Red flagging** The process by which problems and mistakes are discovered early on, before it is too late to remedy them or too late to reduce the cost of the mistakes and problems.

It's easy to see the purposes and functions of a set of house plans. You'd probably call it common sense, because it's so obvious. Yet, when we come to performance, many people lose this common sense and don't realize that building performance is very much like building a house. The planning is critical.

From House Plans to Performance Plans

Let's build on the house analogy and apply it to performance.

First, what's our goal? We want to build a house as efficiently as possible and we want the features and qualities we've chosen for the best cost. Don't we really want the same things with performance? We want to "engineer" performance in the same way. We want employees to function as efficiently as possible, so they contribute as best they can to the success of the organization. To contribute to the organization, we need employees to do the right things (analogous to the house features) and we want them to do those things to a certain level of expertise (standards or specifications).

In talking about the house planning process, I suggested that having the plan allows us to organize the resources necessary to build the house efficiently. What's the parallel with performance? A performance plan allows us to do exactly the same things. If you know what an employee needs to do in the coming year, you can, *at that point*, identify the resources he or she needs to achieve that goal. For example, an employee might need some additional equipment, new skills, or managerial help to clear barriers. The nature of the resources may be different in the two examples, but the principle is the same. Performance planning improves performance simply by virtue of the process of coordinating and allocating resources.

Helping the Employee
By undertaking performance planning, you as manager focus not only on what the employee must do, but also on what you can do to help him or her achieve the designated goals. Focus on both and look for ways to clear the way for success by coordinating activities, providing needed resources, and helping the employee anticipate performance barriers.

The house plan is also a guide or roadmap to the process of building. Once the outcomes or results are designated, it's much easier to plan and to monitor the building process as it goes on. The carpenter can look at drawings or specifications and know from his or her experience in what sequence things must be done. Of course, the plan doesn't specify things like construction sequence or how to actually build the objects, but in the hands of a skilled carpenter it gets pretty close. It's really no different with performance planning. Once it's done, the employee knows where he or she needs to get to and, in the hands of an experienced and expert employee, the plan directly suggests what must get done and in what order. There's a very practical benefit here. Skilled employees with clear goals need significantly less ongoing supervision. They are much better able to self-monitor and self-correct, which is exactly what we want from our employees.

As with the house plan, the performance plan allows better evaluation of progress throughout the actual process and at the end, since both parties have agreed on what is required and how well it is to be done. This makes it *much* easier at the review end, because there should be much less argument about whether the employee has hit the targets, if they've been clearly designated.

Summing Up the Value of Performance Plans

There is no question that if you are doing performance reviews and *not* doing performance planning, you are guaranteed to lose almost all of the value you could gain by doing both. In fact, in some situations, doing reviews without planning can be harmful. Reviewing performance in situations where the employee never had a clear idea of what he or she was expected to do (note the past tense) is bound to cause friction and frustration between employee and manager.

Unfortunately, many of the review tools (outlined in Chapters 4 and 5) don't demand of managers that they plan performance properly. The most common method, the rating approach, only requires sitting down with employees and rating them along various, usually vague dimensions. You can do the rating without any performance planning—and that's what most managers do. They are actually led astray by the ratings systems provided to them and, since most people work on the principle of least effort, they do only what is required.

Here's a very key point. Regardless of the review system you are given, whether it's ratings or rankings or objectives, you *must* do performance planning to make things work. Doing proper performance planning can transform an abominable review system into something of value, if you commit to it.

Communicate Throughout the Year ⚠️ **CAUTION!**

The benefits you gain from performance planning will be lost unless you make a conscious effort to make sure there is ongoing communication about performance throughout the year. Don't assume the planning process stands by itself. It forms the basis for both ongoing communication and performance reviews, which are both required to gain maximum benefits.

By the End of Performance Planning ...

We have two more tasks to complete in this chapter. We need to describe in detail where you and the employee will be by the conclusion of the performance planning process. Then we need to look at how to get it done.

Let's begin by examining what outcomes and results will be created once performance planning is complete. Knowing where we need to go with planning will help us figure out exactly how to go about it.

The Employee

Where should the employee be at the conclusion of the performance-planning phase? Keeping in mind that planning is used to maximize performance and to lay a foundation for ongoing communication and the review process, here's the answer.

By the conclusion of the planning phase the employee should know:

- The most important job responsibilities that he or she needs to complete
- When he or she must complete the job tasks (if appropriate)
- How those job responsibilities relate to the goals of the work unit and the company
- How well or to what "level" he or she needs to perform the job activities
- The criteria that will be used to review performance during and at the end of the review period
- Potential barriers to performing the job tasks and possible solutions
- Any assistance to be expected from the manager toward performing appropriately and overcoming possible performance barriers

Those are the "hard" outcomes related to the employee's understanding of his or her job and expectations about the job. There's a little more to this, though. There are other outcomes—"soft" outcomes that don't relate directly to getting the job done. These have to do with how the employee perceives the whole process and the relationships between himself or herself and the manager and, by extension, the company.

Why is this important? Because we need to pay attention not only to the nuts and bolts of the job in question, but also to the motivation and desire of the employee to achieve those goals. When an employee feels manipulated by his or her manager, or otherwise feels that the manager and employee are not "on the same side," it's likely that the desire to do a good job will decrease. If this occurs and the decline is unchecked, it creates a climate where performance problems arise. So, in addition to the "hard" job-related outcomes listed previously, let's add a few "soft" ones.

> **Creating Soft Outcomes**
>
> **TRICKS OF THE TRADE**
>
> It's far easier to build good employee-manager relationships and trust during the performance-planning phase than to ignore relationships until you reach the performance review phase. That's because performance planning is a far less threatening process to most people. If you create the "soft" outcomes in planning, you will have them in place when you need them during the review process.

By the end of the performance-planning process, the employee should:

- Have the sense that the manager is more interested in creating success than in finding fault later.
- Feel that the manager is willing to help the employee.
- Feel that the manager recognizes that the employee has significant knowledge and ability to increase productivity and achieve greater success in his or her job.
- Have a sense that he or she and the manager are on the same wavelength and share similar goals and concerns (being on the same side).

If you achieve both these hard and soft outcomes during planning, you'll be amazed at how little time you need to spend throughout the year and during the review process.

The Manager

Where does the manager need to be at the conclusion of the planning phase? By the end of the process, the manager should:

- Better understand the employee's day-to-day job responsibilities.
- Have a clear idea of how carrying out those responsibilities contributes to the work unit.
- Be confident that both he or she and the employee have a *shared* understanding of the job and performance expectations.
- Have dealt with how he or she can help the employee succeed and be committed to any actions required to help the employee.
- Have some documentation of the performance-planning process and decisions made.

Do you notice how few things we've mentioned here, compared with the outcomes listed for the employee? There's a simple explanation.

The point of the entire process, from planning to reviewing, is to help the employee succeed. The logic underlying this is that if each employee succeeds, the work unit succeeds, and if the work unit succeeds, the manager must surely be succeeding. Hence, the planning process focuses on where the employee needs to be and not as much on where the manager needs to be. Lest you think this philosophy is a bit naïve, we should say that there are exceptions to this, which we'll deal with in Chapter 11. There we'll discuss this process as it relates to those employees who exhibit substandard performance.

Step-by-Step Planning Process—Getting It Done

As with performance review meetings, there's no single best way to conduct the performance-planning meeting. The steps described below are meant to serve as a template that you can modify to suit your particular needs.

Preparation

If both employee and manager are well prepared for performance planning, the face-to-face meeting time required to complete the process is reduced drastically. In an age where everyone is expected to "do more with less," this is

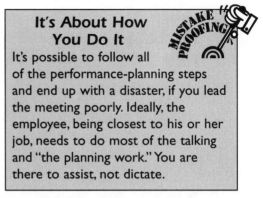

It's About How You Do It

It's possible to follow all of the performance-planning steps and end up with a disaster, if you lead the meeting poorly. Ideally, the employee, being closest to his or her job, needs to do most of the talking and "the planning work." You are there to assist, not dictate.

no trivial issue. After all, we don't want the performance management process to be so time-consuming that the costs outweigh the benefits.

Schedule the Meeting. Your first step is to schedule a meeting time with the employee. At this point you should explain the purpose of the meeting (to plan for the upcoming year), and explain your "working together" philosophy to the employee. You can also specify what if any preparation and meeting pre-work would be useful (see below).

Meeting Pre-Work. We want to move as much of the planning work as possible outside the meeting time, for reasons of efficiency and time management. Here are some possible and very useful pre-work items, for you and/or the employee:

- Review the organization's and work unit's goals for the upcoming year (if available).
- Review the employee's job description.
- Develop tentative goals or objectives for the employee. (Usually the employee can do this.)
- Identify any barriers anticipated that might hinder achievement of these goals.
- Tentatively identify how you can help.

Advanced and veteran employees can do the bulk of the planning on their own. There's no question that the more an employee knows about the company and the work unit, the more work he or she can do outside of the planning meeting. Take the employee's level of understanding into account when asking for pre-work.

Planning Meeting Steps

The duration of the planning meeting and what you need to do during the meeting depend a lot on the work that has been done to prepare for it and the expertise of the employee. In general, the format is as follows.

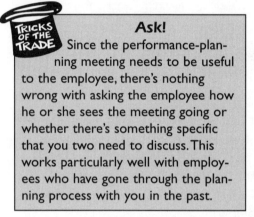

Ask! Since the performance-planning meeting needs to be useful to the employee, there's nothing wrong with asking the employee how he or she sees the meeting going or whether there's something specific that you two need to discuss. This works particularly well with employees who have gone through the planning process with you in the past.

Provide Context

The first step in the planning meeting is to state or reiterate its purpose. Generally the manager gives a short explanation that includes the following points:

- The purpose: Why we are doing this?
    - To make sure the work you do lines up with what the work unit needs to do
    - To create a shared understanding of the expectations about your job
    - To ensure we can red flag problems early if they occur
    - To have some frame of reference when it's time to review performance
    - To update your job description (if that's important).
- The sequence of the meeting:
    - Outline the steps you will follow for the meeting (as per this section).
    - Explain your attitude to the process (e.g., an opportunity for us to work together, a chance to look at resources you need to do your job).

- How the information will be used:
  - How the plan will provide the basis for performance review
  - How the plan will allow the employee to self-monitor and red flag

Give an Overview of Organization and Work Unit Goals

Discuss the organization's and work unit's priorities and concerns for the next year, with special focus on what the work unit needs to accomplish. This is an important link, since each employee's goals and objectives should be determined with reference to the overall strategy and expectations of the work unit. Sometimes the information is available on paper and can be reviewed prior to the meeting. If not, you should offer a brief overview.

Identify Current Job Tasks

You can begin the discussion by asking the employee to explain what he or she is doing currently—the job tasks, where the most time is spent, and how those tasks link up with the work-unit's goals. You may find some things the employee should no longer be doing.

Identify Needed Changes

Explore any changes and additions to the employee's job responsibilities and day-to-day activities that result from the work unit's goals. After you do this, you should end up with a set of specific job tasks the employee keeps, some that may be eliminated, and some new ones. As with much of this process, you should be asking questions of the employee, rather than dictating.

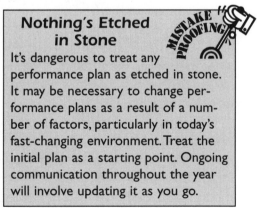

Nothing's Etched in Stone

It's dangerous to treat any performance plan as etched in stone. It may be necessary to change performance plans as a result of a number of factors, particularly in today's fast-changing environment. Treat the initial plan as a starting point. Ongoing communication throughout the year will involve updating it as you go.

Establish Performance Criteria

Once you have a list of job tasks and responsibilities, you need to address how well each should be done. In a management-by-objectives scheme, this would involve writing out standards of performance. Performance criteria should be measurable and as objective as possible, but what's really important is that, by the end of the meeting, both you and the employee have similar expectations about what constitutes "good" performance versus "poor" performance. No matter what techniques you're going to use to review performance—ratings, narratives, 360-degree feedback—you *should* discuss performance criteria.

Before we move on to the next step, we need to address how rewards, such as pay raises or promotions, should be handled. Companies have very different mechanisms to reward their better employees. Some even lack a merit pay system. Of the companies that have merit increases, the large majority of them decide who is deserving of reward during the review process at the end of every review period. That's not an insurmountable problem, except that the criteria used to reward employees are often "concocted" at the point of review. In other words, many employees go through an entire year completely unaware of what they need to do to receive that extra reward, finding out only at the "end of the line." This creates a number of serious problems and it's one reason why performance reviews have such a bad reputation and are often unpleasant.

It also removes the *incentive factor* for employees. Rewards serve as an incentive only when employees know in advance what they must do to receive the reward. If they don't know the expectations and criteria, they're not likely to feel very motivated to go after it.

What you need to know right now is that part of establishing performance criteria is making sure you and the employee agree that if he or she achieves certain goals, there will be a reward. Ideally, the specifics about the reward (e.g., salary increase, promotion, perks) should also be available to the employee as a

result of the performance-
planning process.

It's not always possible
to do that. We'll return to
this crucial topic in
Chapter 10.

Identify Barriers and Required Resources

Let's recap. You've identified job responsibilities and
tasks by linking them to
organizational goals and
specified criteria for per-
formance. Now, you address the following questions:

> **Making The Best of ...**
> **Smart Managing**
>
> You probably are not in control of how rewards are distrib-uted in your company, so that means you have to work within the system you are given. That means you may have to compromise and use an approach that you know is less than perfect. Make the best of it. You can explain that to the employee, so it's clear that you have limits on what you can do.

- What barriers to achieving the goals are anticipated?
- How can those barriers be overcome or their effects reduced?
- What can you do to help?
- What additional resources are needed to "hit the targets"?

Develop Action Plans

Action planning involves getting very specific about who needs to do what and when it should be done. For example, if you have promised to secure some specific resources to help the employee meet his or her goals, during action planning you'd specify the steps you will follow to do that and any relevant timeline.

If the employee works on specific projects, he or she might develop a timetable and an action plan that maps out the steps needed to reach the overall project goal (almost like project management).

Actions plans are very important, but may not fit all jobs and all circumstances. They fit best for project-based jobs or to describe non-routine actions that are required to reach the goal.

Don't Micro Plan

It's possible to create action plans of such detail that the whole process becomes more trouble than it's worth. Create action plans of sufficient detail to guide you and/or your employee, but don't create them when the actions are simple. Don't require an employee to write out action plans for every one of his or her tasks.

Document the Discussion

The performance-planning discussions are important in themselves. However, it's important to document the discussions and agreements for future reference. The document need not be lengthy; in fact, it should be as short as possible. It should include the major job tasks, any criteria or standards agreed upon, and any action plans created. It is this documentation that you're going to use during the review process *and* during ongoing discussions about performance that take place throughout the year.

At this point you may also want to formally change any outdated job description items so they more accurately reflect your discussions.

Ending

At this point you are done. It's a good idea to express any positive feelings you may have about how the meeting has gone and reiterate a small number of the key points. It's always good to thank the employee.

Manager's Checklist for Chapter 6

❏ The performance plan is the foundation of the entire performance review and improvement process. For that reason, it's best to invest your time to do it properly and not cut corners.

❏ The value in planning performance comes from two things—the communication process and the plan that's created. Don't sacrifice one for the other.

❏ Both employee and manager play active roles in the planning process. When possible, the employee should be the primary resource and the manager should not "dictate."

❑ To be useful, the performance review requires performance planning. To be most effective, performance planning requires ongoing communication throughout the year.

❑ It's easier to create a climate of trust between manager and employee during performance planning than during performance reviews. Make that climate creation one of your goals for performance planning.

Review Meetings, Step by Step

There's no single "right way" to conduct a performance review meeting. How you conduct the meeting depends on the kind of system or documentation forms given to you by your company. For example, if you are required to use and complete rating scale forms, the meetings may be a bit different than if you are required to use some sort of narrative format. Regardless, we can identify some guiding principles and steps to take you through the process. There may not be a single right way to do things, but there are some principles that apply to *all* performance review meetings. You need to do the following:

- Make sure the employee understands the purpose of the meeting and what the information is to be used for.
- Communicate the message that you and the employee are on the same side and you are focused on working *with* the employee and not doing something *to* the employee.
- Share with the employee the responsibility of evaluating his or her performance.

- Draw the employee into active discussion. In fact, the employee should be doing most of the talking throughout the meeting.
- Comply with any requirements set forth by your company (e.g. completing a set of forms provided) while trying to make the review process useful to you and the employee.

By the end of the performance review, here's what you should have accomplished:

- Confirmed the major job responsibilities of the employee.
- Provided the employee with your observations and suggestions regarding his or her performance.
- Received comments and suggestions from the employee as to how the two of you can work together to improve performance.
- Identified barriers in the system that need to be overcome and agreed on how that will be done.
- Completed any forms or other paperwork required of you by your company.
- Documented any decisions and/or discussions and recommendations about pay, promotion, or disciplinary action.

Generally we can divide the performance review meeting into the following steps.

1. Warm up and clarify expectations and roles for the meeting.
2. Describe and review the main job tasks and responsibilities.
3. Elicit input from the employee.
4. Discuss and negotiate.
5. Engage in performance improvement problem-solving.
6. Decide on what to record.
7. Finish and plan for follow-up.

> **Watch the Time** TRICKS OF THE TRADE
>
> It's important that performance review meetings don't go on so long that you and the employee get fatigued. You don't have to finish the review process in one sitting. If the meeting goes longer than 90 minutes, it's too long.

Warm Up and Clarify Expectations and Roles

There's usually some initial discomfort or anxiety at the start of every performance review meeting. As the manager, your responsibility is to create a climate in which constructive conversations can occur so you and the employee can become partners in the performance improvement process. That's your first priority. You start the process when you set up the performance review meeting and then continue it when the employee walks through the door. Think of it like warming up for a tennis match or a run. You can't go from a dead stop to full speed with your body, and you can't do that mentally either.

There are two parts to the process. First there's a "putting at ease" step, a warm-up. Second, there's the process of clarifying expectations for the meeting and clarifying your role and that of the employee, so you are both on the same wavelength.

Warm Up

Performance review meetings start with what some might call small talk. A simple "How are you doing?" is a good start, or some neutral, even bland discussion of unimportant topics. It's important that you keep the small talk brief. If it goes on too long, it may make the employee more anxious, and we don't want that. Does that sound silly or phony to you? Remember that almost all social interactions begin with easy topics and the basic social amenities. Small talk isn't artificial, but a genuine way to begin conversations and dialogue.

After a few minutes of chitchat, move to surface any feelings or thoughts the employee has about the review process. The reasoning is simple. If the employee has anxieties, fears, or other reactions that can get in the way of real, constructive dialogue, you need to know. Although you can sometimes tell these things from the employee's behavior, behavior isn't always a reliable indicator.

You need to ask. After the initial small talk, that's what you do. Here's one way of phrasing it: "So, John, how are you feeling about this meeting? Looking forward to it or a bit nervous?" Here's another phrase: "Most of us feel a little uncomfortable about these review meetings. How are you doing right now?" Yet another way of doing it is to share your own feelings about the meeting; for example: "I always feel uncomfortable at the start of these meetings, but it fades fast. How are you doing?"

Listen to what the employee has to say and make it "OK to be uncomfortable." When necessary, reassure the employee if he or she brings up specific worries or concerns and focus on the meeting's purpose—you and the employee work-ing *together.*

You accomplish several things here. First, you set the stage for dialogue and get across the idea that the meeting isn't about you doing something *to* the employee. Second, you allay any specific concerns on the part of the employ-ee as best you can. Just

> **Anticipate Anxiety**
>
> **Smart Managing**
>
> Don't assume that an employee is comfortable with the review meeting. Check it out. Be alert for signs of discomfort or frustration, not only at the beginning of the meeting but throughout the meeting. You aren't there to do thera-py, but when emotions block progress, then it's best to surface them.

don't expect that a few minutes at the beginning of the meeting is going to put employees perfectly at ease.

Clarify Expectations and Roles

While the warm-up is an important beginning, the clarification of roles and expectations is probably more critical. Part of the anxiety surrounding performance reviews is that the employee doesn't know what to expect. What questions go through the employee's head?

Here are a few that you need to answer early on:

- What do you expect from me during the meeting?
- What can I expect from you?
- Are you going to lecture, scold, or harm me?
- What's the point of all this?
- How do the results affect my future or my pay?

Meeting Setup Checklist

When setting up the performance management review meeting, this is what should be discussed.

- The purpose, including benefits to the employee
- How the process will work (focusing on employee input and control)
- Your intent to ensure "no surprises"
- Time, place, and length expected
- Need to arrange uninterrupted time
- Any work employee should do (and you also will do) before the meeting

As I mentioned earlier, there are two points in time where you clarify expectations: first when you set up the performance review appointment and then at the start of the performance review meeting. Let's begin with setting up the appointment.

When you set up the performance review meeting with the employee, it's important to explain the point of the meeting, what to expect, and anything the employee can do prior to the meeting to make the process easier. For example, one common pre-meeting activity is to have the employee review his or her job description to see if he or she thinks it is still accurate or needs revision; doing this in advance results in shorter review meetings. Or, you might request that the employee review any documentation that was produced during the performance planning meetings you undertook at the beginning of the review period. If the performance planning was done properly and both you and the employee review those discussions prior to the review meeting, the entire process will be much smoother. You might ask the employee to think about how he or she did during the year on particular projects and to write down any stumbling blocks or barriers to performance he or she encountered. When both parties prepare well for the meeting, it reduces the stress and uncertainty associated with the performance review and can shorten the review meetings significantly. Preparation is one of the keys to keeping review meetings short.

Here's a sample of how to go about putting expectations on

the table when you make the meeting appointment or when the employee arrives at the meeting.

Mary, let's go over what we are here to accomplish and how I see the meeting going. Nothing is etched in stone, so if you have any suggestions or questions, let me know. What's important here is that we're on the same wavelength so we can work together.

First, as I mentioned when we scheduled this meeting, our main purpose here is to look at your performance over the last year, look at what's going well and identify any areas where we can work together to help you improve over the next year. Another thing we have to do is finish the annual paperwork so there's an official record of our conversation, in case it's needed if you are up for a promotion or pay raise. We're not here to pick at you or find fault or even to find someone to blame for things that have gone wrong. In any event, I don't have anything to say to you that we haven't already talked about in the last year, so I guarantee there won't be any surprises for you.

What we are going to do is review your job tasks and responsibilities and I'm going to ask you to tell me the most important job responsibilities you have. That's just to make sure we understand your job in the same way.

Then I'm going to ask you your opinion of how you've done in the areas we need to discuss. We do that for two reasons—first, to get a sense of what you've accomplished, and second, to identify any areas where you feel you might be able to improve.

We have some other tasks, like doing the paperwork, and I'll go over that when we get there. What you are going to find a bit different is that not only are we going to talk about what you can do to improve your performance, but we're also going to talk about what I can do to help you do that.

So, before we start, does that make sense? Do you have any questions?

Of course, you can modify how you clarify roles and expectations to reflect your own process and style. Pay special atten-

TRICKS OF THE TRADE

The Most Important Thing—Reassurance

The most important thing you can do early on to make this process work is to prove to the employee that the performance review meeting is not going to contain *any* surprises. That means it's absolutely essential to communicate throughout the whole year so there are no surprises and then, of course, to make sure there are *never* any surprises.

tion to the tone of the message and make sure you abide by the expectations you communicate. You can't promise to rely on an employee's suggestions, then reject them out of hand if the employee offers any. In other words, this is one of those situations where you need to walk the talk. Nothing will destroy the review process faster than violating your own expectations.

Describe and Review the Main Job Tasks and Responsibilities

Now it's time to get right into the review process. The first step—discuss the major job tasks and responsibilities the employee has been carrying out in the past year. Jobs change and evolve considerably, even over a single year. A lot of the changes are small and occur almost continuously, so it's quite possible the person is actually doing something quite different from what he or she was doing a year ago, but the changes have never been fully documented. You want to be able to credit the employee for what he or she has achieved, even if it's not in the job description, provided it's a valuable contribution. That's why you start with what the person does and not with the job description. Discussing what the employee *really* does is important so you have a shared idea of the job. Regardless of what kind of form you are asked to use or what kind of evaluation system is required, you should *always* go through this step.

If you and the employee have reviewed the summaries of the performance-planning meeting you had earlier in the year, this process goes much more smoothly. Most of the major job tasks the employee has been carrying out during the year should be listed in the performance-planning documents.

By the end of this step, you should have discussed the following:

- What the employee actually did during the review period.
- Relative importance of the major job responsibilities and job tasks—the most important, the next important, and so on.
- How the person's job tasks link up with or contribute to achieving the company's (or work unit's) goals and objectives.
- Whether the job has changed over the past year and if job descriptions need updating.

When you've finished this step, you will have accomplished two things. You and the employee will have reached agreement on the nature of his or her job, its main job tasks, and the relative importance of those job tasks. This is also the time to put the employee's job responsibilities within the context of what the work unit and the company needed to accomplish. This is very important. Each job task should have a greater purpose—and both you and the employee should agree on why each job task is important.

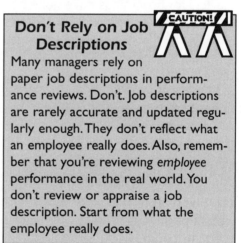

Don't Rely on Job Descriptions

Many managers rely on paper job descriptions in performance reviews. Don't. Job descriptions are rarely accurate and updated regularly enough. They don't reflect what an employee really does. Also, remember that you're reviewing *employee* performance in the real world. You don't review or appraise a job description. Start from what the employee really does.

Elicit Input from the Employee

You'll notice that up to this point you haven't even broached the topic of evaluating, judging, or appraising the employee. That's intentional. What you've done, with the employee, is describe things. You've described the process of the meeting. You've described and clarified job responsibilities with the employee. You've demonstrated you aren't going to be clubbing the employee over the head and you've set a positive tone.

Now it's time to begin the discussion of performance. You're going to do that by first finding out how the employee evaluates his or her job performance over the past time period. The best way to explain this to you is to show you how you might explain this step to the employee. Here's an introduction you might use.

> Tom, now that we're on the same wavelength regarding your job responsibilities, I'd like to get a sense of how you see your accomplishments over the past year and where you've faced issues and problems that have made doing your job more difficult. Since you're the one that knows the most about your job, it makes sense to start with your perceptions. So, I'm going to ask you a few questions. We're not going to write anything down for permanent use at this point, but just get a feel for how things have gone over the last year. After, we'll discuss how we can work together to remove any barriers you may have experienced in getting your work done.
>
> Maybe we can start with your general impression about how things have gone. You can start anywhere, but if you want to talk about the areas where you feel you have done well, that'd be good.

It's the Employee's Turn
During this step, avoid stating your own opinions about the employee's performance. You're going to get your chance to agree or disagree with the employee's perceptions, but let the employee have the first turn. If the employee has difficulty starting, you can help by asking about a particular job responsibility.

Tom gets an opportunity to address this question. At this point, your role is to ask questions and make sure you understand what Tom is saying. Additional questions you might ask include:

- Are there any parts of your job that you feel you could perform better in the next year?

- What kinds of difficulties did you face during the year?

End this step by paraphrasing the main points of the employee's remarks. For example:

So, I'm getting the impression that you are fairly happy with the way things have gone with respect to [job responsibilities], that you feel you really excelled at [job task or specific project], and that you feel there's some room for improvement with ... [Reflect back any comments by the employee on this topic.] Is that accurate?

Clarify to ensure that you have heard what the employee intended to say.

Discuss and Negotiate (Evaluative Component)

Now we get to the part of the meeting where you may encounter difficulties. The first few performance review steps we described so far should not engender any conflict whatsoever, if you have had good performance planning and year-round communication.

If you are not required to make some form of evaluative judgment of the employee's performance, then the entire review process tends to run relatively free of conflicts, including discussion and negotiation, particularly if the employee isn't going to be rewarded or punished based on the results of the review.

That's not usually or often the case. The more riding on the results, the more likely conflict and disagreement will occur—and the more likely the conflict may become unpleasant.

So, you've got an idea of how the employee evaluates his or her performance. What you record for posterity, though, is based on a negotiating process that takes into account both the employee's perceptions and your perceptions. During the discussion and negotiation, you get to present your views. There are two goals. The first is the most obvious and familiar—to move toward agreement about what is to be documented. The second is, in the larger scheme of things, much more important. Once you and the employee have come to some agreements

MISTAKE PROOFING

Leading, Not Telling

Even though you need to share your opinions with the employee, it's better to lead the employee to your opinions by focusing on specific data, events, or observations you have made, then request that the employee take them into account in his or her own "self-evaluation."

on what has gone well and where improvement can take place, then you can problem-solve to determine what needs to be done to improve performance. That's where the real payoff lies.

Since this is the area where you are most likely to encounter difficulties, we'll look at it in greater detail in Chapters 8 and 11. For now, here are some tips and principles.

- Begin with the employee's self-evaluations and offer up your own perceptions linked to them, but keep your comments short.
- Your task is not so much to provide a "final judgment," but to help the employee see his or her performance from another angle, so he or she can "self-assess" more realistically.
- You can state your own perceptions, but it's better to lead the employee somewhat by referencing things you may have observed, measured, or documented and to remind the employee of specific instances that bear closer scrutiny (e.g., a particular customer complaint, high absenteeism).
- Remember: this is a negotiation. First try to come to a mutually acceptable position. Completely overriding an employee's perceptions about his or her performance is a last resort.
- Deal with one issue, job responsibility, or task at a time. Share your perceptions, get feedback and counter-perceptions from the employee, try to come to some agreement, and then move to the next.
- Don't assume the only areas of disagreement will occur

when you feel the employee has done badly and the employee feels he or she has done well. The opposite can occur. Some employees judge their job performances more harshly than you will.

- Focus equally on what the employee has done well and on areas where improvement is indicated. In fact, you will have more success if at least 75% of the discussion and negotiation focuses on what's gone well.
- Try to portray the idea that the meeting purpose is to improve regardless of current levels of performance, and that you work with each staff member in the same way— to improve performance continuously.

We are going to return to this later on and, in particular, help you work effectively when disagreement and problems occur.

Engage in Performance Improvement Problem-Solving

Let's recap where you are in the performance review meeting. You've set a cooperative climate and come to an understanding on how the meeting will proceed. You've reviewed job responsibilities and tasks, their relative importance, and how they contribute to the work unit and the company. You've heard the employee's self-evaluation, shared your own perceptions, and agreed on some areas where you and the employee can work together to improve performance.

What's next? Probably the most important part of the whole meeting.

During the performance improvement problem-solving step, you and the employee work together to answer this question: "What are the barriers to performance improvement, wherever they may lie?" The answers to this simple question enable performance improvement. After all, if you don't know why or how performance has been affected for the worse, how can you go about improving it?

Problem Solving Questions
Here are some good problem-solving questions to use with employees.
- If we could do one thing to help you improve performance, what would it be?
- What's the single biggest thing that slows you down?
- Last summer your production was down while others' went up. Was there something going on then that made your work more difficult?

We'll come back to this in Chapter 8, but by the end of the performance problem-solving process, here is what you'll have accomplished:

- Identified any barriers to performance the employee has faced during the review period.
- Developed strategies for removing them or reducing their negative effects in the present and the future.
- Defined any specific action steps required, whether of you or of the employee, and committed to them.

Decide on What to Record

Since one of our purposes in the review meeting is to complete required forms and document the employee's performance, we need to include this step. It involves going through the forms, whether narrative, rating, or whatever else has been supplied.

You may be wondering why this step comes *after* the performance problem-solving step. Why not do it as part of the negotiation step? Here's why. The final evaluations and judgments you commit to paper need to reflect factors under the control of the employee, taking into account factors not under the control of the employee.

Let's say, for example, that one of the items on a rating form is about whether the employee completes work tasks "on deadline." If you look only at the number of tasks done on time versus those that come in late, the final evaluation may unfairly penalize an employee for things beyond his or her control.

For example, let's say that over the last year your company's suppliers have been consistently late with raw materials and that the responsibility for managing suppliers doesn't rest with your employee, but with another department. As a

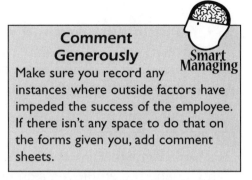

Comment Generously

Smart Managing

Make sure you record any instances where outside factors have impeded the success of the employee. If there isn't any space to do that on the forms given you, add comment sheets.

result, the employee has been consistently late in accomplishing his or her work tasks. If you looked only at "on time" and "late" figures, you might rate the employee much lower than average, when the problem has nothing to do with him or her at all.

So, when you need to document the review, the record needs to reflect both actual results and behavior *and* whether the employee was unable to do his or her job effectively because of things beyond his or her control. To understand how important this is, imagine how an effective employee will feel if he or she is denied a pay increase, criticized, or penalized for something completely beyond his or control. There's no better way to destroy an employee's loyalty, morale, and dedication than to do this. Don't.

This step is also very important; we'll return to it in a later chapter.

Finish and Plan for Follow-Up

You're almost done for now. It's time to wrap up and plan for follow-up. It sounds straightforward enough, simple even, but don't discount the importance of ending the meeting properly. It's not quite that simple. Here is what you need to accomplish by the end of this step:

- Both you and the employee need to sign off on any documentation of the performance review meeting.
- You summarize (recap) the results and the nature of the discussions to make sure you and the employee have similar perceptions of the meeting.

- You uncover any emotional reactions the employee may have.
- You and the employee agree on any follow-up steps, including getting ready for the next round of performance planning and actions needed by either or both parties.

The Sign-Off Process

Let's begin with the sign-off process. It's very important that both you and the employee sign any documentation for the review meeting—but not for the reason you think. The signatures indicate that you and the employee have been parties to the communication process and that the employee acknowledges having communicated with you about performance. It does *not* mean and *should* not mean that the employee *agrees* 100% with the final result. It's simply an acknowledgment that the process has taken place. The form you use should reflect that. For example, it might have something like this:

> **TRICKS OF THE TRADE**
>
> **Copies for Everyone**
> After both you and the employee have acknowledged (signed) the documentation material and if it is determined it's the final version, make sure both of you have copies, in addition to any copies sent to the human resources department.

I [employee] acknowledge that the contents of this form have been communicated to me and discussed with me on [date] and that I have been provided an opportunity to add my own comments and input.

Why do we need this? If there is any doubt as to whether the employee has been treated fairly and a legal battle results, you may be required to show that you have communicated to the employee any concerns about performance.

Why wouldn't we have the signature indicate agreement to the contents? To be honest, it's probably unreasonable to expect that manager and employee will agree on every detail recorded on the evaluation forms. When there is significant disagreement, some employees will not sign a form that signifies agreement, which then makes the documentation inadequate for legal purposes. The employee *must* understand the meaning of the signature—an acknowledgment the meeting has taken place. In the unlikely event the employee refuses to sign anything, make sure that's indicated on the record. You can suggest that he or she think on it for a day or two; then contact the employee to see if he or she has reconsidered.

Recap and Check Emotional Reactions

You and the employee have gone through a process that tends to cause anxiety for both parties. The recap serves two purposes: to ensure that both parties understand the details of the discussion in the same way and to reinforce the positive process and outcomes of the meeting.

You can recap in one of two ways. You can ask the employee to summarize the key points and what's been accomplished during the meeting or you can do so. Ideally the employee does it, but, and it's a significant *but*, many employees may not be good at doing so. There's really nothing wrong with the manager doing it.

> **Emotions—The Key** **Smart Managing**
>
> Performance appraisals are emotional experiences for employees because they are always a bit uncertain about what to expect and the reviews affect their future. So you need to be sensitive to this, know your employees well, and execute the review in a way that focuses on performance and improvement. This makes the process less personal and more positive for all involved.

You also need to do something else, to check for any emotional reactions that you need to deal with. At the end of your recap, you probably want to ask the employee how he or she feels about the process. The purpose is simple. You want to have the chance to defuse any anger or frustration the employee is feeling; ideally, you need to do that before the employee leaves the meeting.

Here's an example:

Well, John, we're pretty much finished. I think we've accomplished a lot here. We've looked at your job description and brought it up to date. We've identified some of the things that have affected your performance over the last year. We've also identified some things I can do to help you move forward, some opportunities for training for you, and we've finished off the forms for this year.

I'd like to thank you for working with me on this. I know it's a little difficult, but next time it should be a bit easier, since we'll both know what to expect.

We have one more thing to summarize, about what's next, but I'd like to get a sense of how you feel about the meeting. We don't need to get into it too deeply, since I know we're both tired, but are you OK with how the meeting went and where we've finished up?

That's a little short. You may want to provide more detail, hitting the high points of the meeting. If it turns out the employee is upset, you need to decide whether to pursue it directly at that time or to leave it for a day or two. The advantage of dealing with it immediately is that it allows no time for worrying. The disadvantage is that the employee may not be in a state of mind to pursue it just then. You need to use your best judgment.

Plan Follow-Up and Future Action

You can include this in the recap or put it at the end of the step. The purpose is to make sure both you and the employee agree on any commitments, follow-up actions, responsibilities, and so on. Obviously the content is going to depend on how the entire meeting has gone and where you've stopped. It may be necessary to have a second performance review meeting to tie up loose ends or if there are things you and the employee need to think over.

In any event, here's a way to do it:

So, we've agreed that I'm going to see what we can do about addressing the problems with our suppliers, so you won't be handcuffed in the future. I'm also going to [reiterate your commitments]. If you have ideas on how we could get those things done, please let me know as you think of them. We've also agreed that you might benefit from some training on some of the new technologies and both of us will scout out some possibilities there.

We talked about the issue of punctuality and identified some of the causes of that. You've indicated to me that you are going to [action specified] and we will revisit this in a few months to see if we need to do anything else about it.

Now, the forms are completed; they go up to personnel and you have your own copy. In the next month or two, I would like to sit down with you to plan and discuss your job responsibilities for the next year. Since we've covered most of that discussion in this meeting, it should only take about 20 minutes.

Have I missed anything about what we're going to do?

So, there you are. We've covered the basic steps of the performance review process. Remember that the sequence and details can vary a lot and you may need to modify the steps to suit the situation, the forms, and the reactions you receive from the employee. For example, sometimes it makes sense to split the process into two meetings, sometimes not.

Manager's Checklist for Chapter 7

❑ The prime performance review directive: no surprises.

❑ Performance reviews are owned by both employee and manager, so it's important to encourage the employee to be an equal participant. Don't monopolize the conversations.

❑ Rely on the employee to supply basic information about job responsibilities as they really are. Don't use outdated job descriptions.

❑ Make sure you don't focus only on performance problems. Employees also need to know what they've done well so they can continue doing it.

❑ Pay attention to what is said and how things are said. The way the meeting is conducted is just as important as what is said, and perhaps more important.

❑ Both you and the employee need to sign off on any documentation completed as a result of the performance review. The employee's signature doesn't signify agreement, but only acknowledgment that the meeting has taken place.

Diagnosing, Problem Solving, and Ongoing Communication

So far, we've covered the two pieces of bread in the performance management review sandwich. The first piece is performance planning—the starting point for the entire system
used to manage performance. The second piece is the performance review meeting; we've looked at its purpose and how you
should conduct the meeting. Those two pieces are critical, but
not enough in your quest to improve the performance of your
employees, your work unit, and the company, which, after all, is
the point of performance management reviews.

In this chapter we're going to talk about the meat of the
sandwich—that stuff that goes between the planning and the
meeting. We'll help you become more adept at diagnosing the
factors that undermine performance. That's the diagnosis
process. We'll address the problem-solving process, which
involves you and each employee working together to find solutions to improve performance. We'll also give you some practi-

cal help and ideas about how to ensure ongoing communication throughout the whole year.

What Is Diagnosing Performance Issues?

The process of diagnosing performance issues is one of communication and analysis in which you work with the employee to identify factors that interfere with performance.

Here's a very important point. When most people talk about "diagnosing," they tend to use a reactive medical model to guide their thinking. That is, they assume that you "diagnose" when a person or performance is "sick." In fact, some performance management experts use a less neutral term than issues—they talk about "diagnosing performance *problems*." As a result of this kind of thinking, there's a tendency to diagnose performance *only* when there is a glaring, obvious problem.

Smart Managing

Diagnosing for Continuous Improvement

Diagnosis fits whenever there is interest in improving performance, regardless of the current level of performance. Diagnosis is used to address poor performance, help average performers become above average, and help above-average performers become legendary.

It is true that diagnosing is necessary if you want to address poor performance, since to fix the problem, you really do need to know what is causing it. It's necessary to go further if our goal is to maximize productivity across the board. Here's why.

You probably have a good number of average performers. Average performers, by definition, don't have huge and obvious performance *problems*. They do their jobs, but they aren't standouts. If you're committed to improving performance, you need to ask the question: What causes these folks to be performing at an average level? When you know the answer to that question, then it's possible to examine whether the average performers can improve to become superior performers. In other words, diagnosing performance issues involves not only dealing with problems, but also working to identify causes and ways to improve performance for average *and* above-average performers. If you do that, you're much more likely to improve the overall performance of your work unit.

When Do You Do Performance Diagnostics?

It's a bit inaccurate to place diagnosing performance between the two pieces of bread—performance planning and performance reviews. Diagnosing performance can occur at *any* point in time. It should be used all year around, but also *during* the performance review meeting. The reason is simple. You want to catch performance issues as early as possible, diagnose the causes, and address those causes. The sooner you do that, the more likely you are to prevent small issues from growing.

You also need to include the diagnosis process as part of your performance review meetings. The most apparent reason to do so is so you can address performance issues during the meeting so things get better during the next review period or the next year.

There's another, less obvious reason why performance diagnostics must occur during performance reviews. Recall that performance reviews work best when oriented toward the present and the future, rather than focusing on the past. You may recall that we mentioned that a "no blaming" philosophy is important, so that employee and manager can work together. Including the performance diagnostics process in the performance review meeting helps to remind both you and the employee of the main purpose of the performance review—to improve performance. When done properly, it conveys the message that manager and employee can work together to achieve common goals. Inclusion moves the review process from a problematic appraisal and evaluation process, which tends to be threatening, to an improvement process, which is far less threatening.

Guiding Principles

We know that diagnosing performance issues works best when you follow some relatively straightforward principles and guidelines. Let's take a look at them.

Talking Too Much?
If you're trying to diagnose performance issues and you end up doing most of the talking, you can be fairly sure the process has gone off the rails. Avoid the common pitfall of telling the employee what's causing the performance issue. Lead the employee to examine performance issues for himself or herself.

Employee Focus. The person in the best position to identify barriers to performance and reasons why they occur is the person who does the job. That means the diagnostic process should focus on the wisdom of the employee, with the manager playing a guiding role to "tease out" the causes behind performance issues. That doesn't mean that you have to accept what the employee says, but only that you start with the employee. Besides, whenever possible, you want to encourage the employee to self-diagnose.

Root Causes. To improve performance, we need to go beyond our initial diagnostic opinions. Too often the real causes or barriers to performance lie underneath the superficial ones. So we need to distinguish between the superficial causes—those that are easily seen but not as important as they first appear—and the root causes—those that lie beneath and are the real reasons for performance issues.

Types of Causes. There are two major types of causes behind performance issues. The first type has to do with employee characteristics. As we described in Chapter 3, employee-based factors include employee skill levels, motivation, ability, training, and so on. It's common for that to be the focus of most diagnostics. The second type of causes has to do with the system in which work is done. Again, as we pointed out in Chapter

3, the environment in which the employee works affects performance: managerial behavior, allocation of resources, colleagues, and a wide range of other variables. Managers tend to overlook these "systems factors." That's bad, because often the more obvious employee variables are superficial causes, while the root causes are in the work environment or the system in which the employee works. So, shift the focus to system variables, rather than concentrating on flaws in the employee.

How Do You Do It?

The best way to understand the diagnostic process is through an example. Let's take the case of Martha, the manager, and Tom, the receptionist and switchboard operator. The process of diagnosing would be the same for any job type—for a consultant, for a factory worker, or any other job.

The following dialogue takes place during the performance review meeting, but something similar could take place any time throughout the year. We join the conversation after an initial discussion of some data that suggests there are some areas where Tom both could and needs to improve his performance.

Martha: So, we both agree that customers are having to spend a lot of time on hold, and they aren't getting their questions answered in a prompt manner, since we have some feedback from customers about this, right?

Tom: Yes. As we discussed, my role in the department is to be the first customer contact person, and I can certainly see that if customers get annoyed about the first contact, we're losing business. (Note that Tom is indicating an understanding of where his work "fits," because he and Martha discussed it earlier in the review meeting.)

Martha: Yes, that's true. Your role is very important here. OK, have you got any idea why the customers are experiencing long wait times? (Martha is following our first guideline—the one we called "employee focus.")

Tom: I'm not exactly sure. There are a bunch of things that are possible. I often have to put people on hold when I'm trying to route their calls to the right staff member. Sometimes I don't know who to send the call to or I don't know if the person is available to take the call. Other times I'm dealing with irate customers who haven't had their calls returned or who get rerouted to me when they hit voice mail. That takes a lot of my time, so I can't get to the other calls quickly.

Martha: I think you're on to something here, Tom. Let's look at these things one by one. You said you don't know who to route the calls to. Why is that happening? (Martha is using a tool called the Five Why's that we'll detail later in the chapter.)

Importance of Climate

Performance diagnostics and problem solving simply don't work in an adversarial climate or where the employee sees the manager as the enemy. If you find employees who are hesitant to be open with you, consider the possibility that your own managerial behavior is such that it has eroded trust.

Tom: Well, things change a lot around here from week to week. People's responsibilities seem to change on a weekly basis. And for some reason, nobody thinks to tell me when those things change. I want to try to get the customer to the right person the first time, so I need to ask someone and that means putting the customer on hold. I don't know why nobody tells me stuff.

Martha: So you are really describing two things here. One is that things change a lot and change fast, and the other is that you aren't getting the information you need to do your job effectively, right? (Tom nods.) So, why do you figure people aren't giving you that information? (Again, Martha is using the Five Why's tool.)

Are you seeing the pattern here? Martha relies on Tom's experience to figure out where the problems lie. She doesn't stop at the first level of cause, but continues to dig to find the cause underneath the cause, so she can identify root causes.

If the root causes aren't examined, the problem can't be fixed. Pay special attention to the tone—don't accuse and don't blame—and focus on causes that are part of the work environment.

In the example, it's clear that Martha could send Tom for additional training on how to operate the switchboard, or provide bonus pay, or threaten and cajole, and yet performance could not possibly improve because she would not be addressing the real problem. That's not to say Tom's skills, ability, work habits, and so forth are off limits. It may be that performance can be improved by addressing those factors *in addition* to looking at the system causes.

The example we've given is only a short segment, but the pattern would be repeated for any and all of the other issues Tom has identified. Martha can also offer her opinions

> ### No Blame
> The quickest way to destroy th[e] [diag]nostic process is to sound blaming or accusatory. Remember that it doesn't matter *who* is at fault or to blame for anything in the past. What's important to figure out is *why* something went wrong to make sure it doesn't happen again. Your goal isn't to pin the tail on the donkey.

of possible causes for the performance issue. The starting point, however, is Tom's perceptions.

We're going to come back to this dialogue shortly as we extend the diagnostic process into the problem-solving process. Before we do that, here's an important tool you can use to move beyond superficial causes to get at root causes.

The Five Why's

The Five Why's tool is an exceedingly simple tool for moving beyond the first answers you get when you try to identify barriers to performance or causes of performance issues. It's so simple anyone can use it successfully. Here's what it is. You keep asking "Why?" for a minimum of five times or until the question can't be answered any more.

Martha was using it in our example. So, stripping out some of the dialogue, here's how it would go.

Martha: Why do customers have to wait on hold for so long?

Tom: Because I don't know if I can route a call to the right person.

Martha: Why don't you know where to route the call?

Tom: Because sometimes I don't know if a person is in or taking calls.

Martha: Why don't you know if a person is in or taking calls?

Tom: Because people don't seem to keep me informed.

Martha: Any idea why people aren't keeping you informed?

Tom: *I* have no idea. Well, maybe ... I guess people don't think I'm important.

That's how it works. This example may sound a bit abrupt, like a rapid exchange of questions and answers, because we've taken out other parts of the dialogue. You don't want the Five Why's to sound like an inquisition as you probe for root causes.

By the end of this example, it's clear that one of the reasons why customers are ending up on hold is that Tom isn't getting the information he needs. This cause is something that's probably beyond Tom's control. Perhaps Tom could do some things to help the situation, but the major source lies with the lack of timely information. To eliminate the problem, Martha needs to take some responsibility for addressing the problem.

Here's another interesting observation. If Martha and Tom duplicate this technique with other possible causes, at the end of the chain for each contributing cause they'll discover the same root cause—a lack of timely information. When you get to the same place from several starting points in a Five Why's dialogue, you can be fairly certain you are at a root cause.

OK, so now what? As with all the parts of the larger performance management system, diagnosis can't stand on its own. Now we get to problem solving, to planning a strategy to remove the barriers or address the causes.

Problem Solving to Remove Barriers

When you diagnose performance, your goal is to identify the reasons why performance is less than it can be. Once you've identified some possible causes, then what? Simple. You remove the barriers you and the employee have identified and see if performance levels change. So, first you find possible causes for performance problems and then you work to remove the barriers. As with our discussion of diagnostics, the best way to grasp this problem-solving process is to continue our dialogue between Martha and Tom.

In our example, the dialogue between Martha and Tom indicated that a major factor limiting Tom's ability to deal with customers quickly on the phone was that he lacked some critical information that would let him route and process calls efficiently. Martha and Tom identified several problems,

> **You Never Know**
>
> You can never be absolutely sure you've nailed the cause of a performance issue or identified the proper remedy. For this reason, view the diagnosis and solutions that come from these discussions as tentative hypotheses. Diagnose, identify possible solutions, implement, and then pay attention to see if things get better. If not, start over.

Smart Managing

none of which Tom could solve by himself. Tom lacked information about who was available to answer customer queries and responsibilities changed so that Tom didn't know to whom he should direct specific calls.

Continuing to use the Five Why's, Martha realized that part (just part) of the reason Tom couldn't do his job more efficiently was that Martha wasn't effectively managing flows of information throughout the organization and, in particular, wasn't handling communication about changes well enough. This was actually confirmed during other meetings with other staff. Let's join the problem-solving process in progress.

Martha: Well, Tom it looks like there are some barriers here that I can try to clear away for you, and there are definitely some things I can do personally to help you so you have the information you need. Before we discuss any of my ideas, do you have any thoughts about how we can solve these problems?

Tom: Well, it's not really my place to say what other people should do. (This is a common response, particularly from people who have jobs lower down in the organization.)

Martha: Let's just brainstorm. Let's not be worried about what other people might think, or even if some solutions seem silly. This is just between us anyway, right now.

Tom: OK. Well, it would really help if we had some kind of board I could refer to or maybe a computer program that could tell me who is available to take calls from customers.... I mean, we have the in/out board, but that doesn't tell me if someone's in a meeting or available or not.

Martha: I think something like that is an excellent idea! It would help me too, so I know who is available if I need someone. I'll tell you what: why don't you think about this a bit more and explore whether it would be better to have a manual board or some kind of simple computer system. You're good at that stuff. Then get back to me with a recommendation. Oh, you might want to talk to other staff, too, to get their ideas. (Notice that Martha involves Tom in the identification and creation of a solution. There are a lot of reasons to do so, but one of the most important is to convey the idea that he is expected to be part of any solution, and not simply identify how others are causing him problems.)

Tom: I can do that. Can I come to you for help?

Martha: Sure, no problem. (At this point the commitment would be sealed by establishing a time by which Tom would get back to Martha. The two continue to explore other possible solutions, but let's skip ahead.)

Martha: Now it seems to me that I need to revisit some of the ways I've been communicating to people about all the changes recently. I need some time to think about my own role here and what I can do to get you the information you need. If you have any suggestions about what I can do, I'd like to hear them now, or after you've had time to think. (Here Martha is acknowledging she has some role in the fixing process. She and Tom then briefly discuss possibilities. Again we skip ahead.)

Martha: Tom, we've talked about how the system isn't helping you do your work and some of the things I might be able to do to help you, but we haven't talked yet about any things you can do to help yourself. One thing I've noticed is that you don't always have information at "the tip of your tongue" that you need to have and that you've been told about. A lot of times you aren't given what you need, but sometimes it seems when you have been informed about some changes, you forget. Do you think that happens?

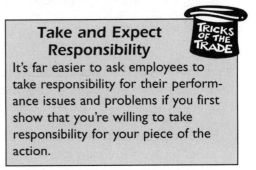

Take and Expect Responsibility

It's far easier to ask employees to take responsibility for their performance issues and problems if you first show that you're willing to take responsibility for your piece of the action.

Tom: Sure, I guess I'm like everyone, sometimes I forget. Do you have anything specific in mind?

Martha: Yes, I think you aren't quite conversant enough with how all the parts of our department link up and work together. That might be one reason you can't answer some of the questions customers pose. Do you think that's accurate? And if so, any ideas how we can get you up to speed?

Tom: That's possible. I never really thought of it before. How about if you give me an hour or two away from the phones for the next few weeks and I can read through the information you want me to remember?

Martha: We can do that, Tom. So let's make a deal. I can free you up for an hour a week on Fridays for the next few weeks, provided you promise to use some of your own time to bone up. Does that sound fair?

Tom: I guess I can do that. I always have some spare time at lunch.

Martha: OK, great. Then that's what we'll do. How about if we talk in a couple of weeks and we'll test you on some of the material? I know that's scary, but again, it's only the two of us, and it will give you a chance to ask me any questions about the company and department that come to mind.

Tom: Sounds good.

The problem-solving process to remove barriers to performance can happen any time. But regardless of the timing, let's map out a few key points you can apply.

- Keep the discussion as employee-centered as possible. The process is a cooperative one that should draw the employee in as an active participant. You have a part of the responsibility for solving problems, but whenever possible lead the employee through the process.
- Cover solutions that are system-based, manager-based (the things you can do to help), and *then* employee-based. The reason to do that is to make sure you don't get locked into looking only at employee-based causes of problems.
- Establish firm commitments on actions needed, whether things that you will do or things the employee will do. That means setting dates and, of course, it means keeping those commitments.

- Don't force solutions. It's not always possible to find solutions at that point in time. It's OK to agree to meet again after collecting information, consulting other people, or doing other things necessary to plan possible solutions.

Ongoing Communication

Probably the most commonsense part of the overall process we're describing has to do with communicating with employees throughout the year. Despite the fact that this is the simplest part of the process and the easiest (not that the other parts are that hard), it's something a lot of managers skip, particularly if their own workloads are heavy. These days a lot of managers are expected to have staff responsibilities in addition to their managerial ones. That can make it difficult for managers to pay attention to ongoing communication, but if you ignore it you'll pay a lot in terms of productivity and even your time. Here's why.

Ongoing communication serves a number of purposes. One of the most important is to inform the manager of problems, either big or small, before they become huge or

> **Don't Get Too Micro**
>
> If you communicate with your employees regularly, there's a risk that you'll try to micromanage them or meddle with their work. You *must* guard against this. Most of the time, ongoing communication is just "touching bases," rather than getting into in-depth discussions in which you tell the employee what he or she should be doing differently. If you plan performance properly, there's no need to micromanage.

impact significantly on productivity. So, the year-round communication process functions as a way of red flagging problems. It also allows the manager to coach and develop employees on the job and help them perform better. One other important function is to ensure that no surprises pop up at review time, so the employee always knows where she or he stands and how things are going. This makes the review process much easier and much less threatening and time-consuming.

When you add up the costs of longer, more difficult review sessions, lost opportunities to improve performance throughout the year, and the cost of unmanaged problems, you'll find that investing in ongoing communication is a real bargain. If you prevent one productivity crisis a year by keeping communication going all year, you will easily recoup the time and resources you spent on communicating properly with employees.

So, what's involved? It's dialogue: it's talking *with* each employee rather than talking *at* them. It can be structured and formal, as in having regular written reports or meetings, or it can be informal—a quick visit down the hall for a five-minute "How's it going?" chat, an occasional brief discussion over lunch or a coffee break. It can be all sorts of things, but the bottom line is that you and the employee need to be able to talk about how his or her job is going and anything that comes up on your end that might relate to the person's job or performance.

Informal Methods

If you restrict ongoing communication to formal methods (see next section), such as reports (print or electronic) or formal meetings, you and your employees might perceive this communication process as too time-consuming or unnecessary. There's also the risk that the cost of formal methods begins to outweigh the benefits. Don't forget that costs need to be considered in light of *both* your time and the time your employees spend in ongoing communication. Whether you use more formal methods or not, informal methods are still important.

> **Smart Managing**
>
> ### A Good Sign
>
> When employees initiate informal conversations about performance issues, that's a good sign, for at least two reasons. It means they tend to trust you enough to approach you and they also understand it's important to keep you informed so you can intervene if necessary.

Informal methods of communicating throughout the year are basically brief conversations about how work is going and any changes that might be occurring that affect what work is done and how it is done. These are basically short, apparently off-the-cuff conversations. Either you or your employees can initiate them, although it's primarily your responsibility to do so if they don't.

So, when can these conversations occur? At almost any time. Here are some examples.

- Walk-arounds: you visit your employees informally
- Brief discussions over coffee or at break time
- Impromptu group meetings
- Employee-initiated impromptu meetings: they drop into your office to talk

Making Them Work

You might think that informal meetings are unplanned, almost random occurrences. That's not strictly accurate. They may very well be planned. For example, you might plan to visit briefly with two or three of your staff members each day, so that every week you talk at least a little with each employee about how things are going. To ensure that these kinds of communication opportunities occur, it's best to plan them out in some systematic way.

Informal methods work best when the employee understands that it's part of your job to stay on top of things and part of his or her job to keep lines of communication open. They also work best when employees don't believe you're trying to check up on them or find opportunities to blame them or take control of their jobs away from them. Setting up conditions to be most effective is not difficult.

First, it's important to explain to employees why you'll be talking to them informally. You should phrase your explanation so it's clear that you're there to *help*, and not to control. For example: "It's part of my job to see if there's anything I can do to help you get your job done, so every so often I'll be talking to each of you about how things are going."

The Informal Scrum

One handy group communication method is called the scrum. It involves short impromptu group meetings to talk about a specific job issues applicable to those who are attending. Anyone can call a scrum—manager or employee. Usually a few hours' notice is given.

Second, as with much of the performance management review process, the emphasis should be on asking questions, rather than telling employees how to do the details of their jobs. The exception to this rule is if you are in a situation where it's important that you communicate some changes that will affect the employee's job tasks.

Formal Methods

Formal communication methods are usually much more structured than informal methods. They include regular meetings with individuals or the team and short, periodic, written reports. Formal methods usually yield some sort of documentation (i.e. meeting minutes, summaries, or reports). It's not uncommon for several formal methods to be used in combination—for example, to have each employee submit a monthly status report *plus* meet monthly to discuss progress.

As we indicated earlier, formal methods tend to take more time than informal methods.

Individual Meetings. These meetings are generally scheduled in advance, perhaps once a month, and used to discuss progress toward job objectives and goals. Since they are scheduled, they allow both employee and manager to prepare for them by making notes or, at minimum, thinking about what needs to be discussed. Individual status meetings are often "mini-review meetings" that include problem identification, diagnosis, and problem solving.

Group Meetings. Often used with teams, group meetings are appropriate when the information to be shared is relevant and important for all members of a group and/or when all members of a team should know what's going on with other team members and their job/team responsibilities. In these meetings, it's not uncommon for each team member to do an oral status update, which can include covering things that are going well, accomplishments, and any issues or barriers that have been identified. Another advantage to group meetings is that they allow for involving more people in problem solving, resulting in more creative solutions than might emerge in one-to-one-meetings. The disadvantage of these meetings is time. The larger the group, the longer the meetings and the more work hours used.

Written Reports. You can also use written reports as a mechanism for employees to update you on progress, problems, etc. They're particularly useful when it's important for you to have regular information about progress. For example, if you're required to report to your boss regularly and she or he wants to be kept current, one way to do that is to get short written reports from employees and summarize those for your boss.

It's probably best to use a very simple reporting form. The form might have space for the employee's main job tasks and space to indicate if the task is progressing well or not, if it's on schedule and/or on budget and so forth. This works well for jobs that are project-based.

There's a major limitation in relying *only* on written reports: although they can help identify problems early on, they're not useful in identifying root causes and solutions. Those functions require face-to-face interactions. So, often written reports (perhaps monthly) are used in conjunction with regular meetings, to reduce the need and length of those meetings.

As with informal methods, formal methods work best when employees understand the purposes of the reports or the meetings and you act in ways that prove to them that your intent is to improve performance. In addition, these methods need to be reasonable in terms of the time required, timely, and useful. One way of determining their usefulness is to ask employees directly. If they feel the meetings are not helping them, then you need to reconsider their use.

Manager's Checklist for Chapter 8

❏ If your goal is to improve performance for each employee, your work unit, and the company, you *must* diagnose performance effectively and problem-solve effectively.

❏ Ongoing communication helps you prevent small problems from escalating and allows frequent mid-course corrections as needed, when needed.

❏ Diagnosing performance issues and problem solving works best when employees understand that your purpose is not to control them or blame them, but to help them.

❏ Use the simple Five Why's tool to help you get to root causes. If you don't identify root causes accurately, you won't be able to improve productivity, since your solutions won't address the underlying causes.

❏ Choose ongoing communication techniques based on your particular situation, but make sure the cost of formal approaches does not outweigh the benefits from using those tools.

Essential Communication Skills

In the business world, there's a tendency to take communication skills for granted or to classify them as "soft" skills—somehow less important than technical skills or other more concrete skill areas. That's unfortunate, because the cost of ineffective communication in *any* context can be huge, but the costs are also often hidden from view, at least until one is faced with glaring situations where communication is just awful.

The reality is that good management cannot be divorced from good communications skills. While there are a number of factors that distinguish between a good manager/leader and an ineffective one, the most obvious and most consistent difference lies with communication. Good managers communicate well. So, let's link this to performance reviews and the supporting elements—performance planning, problem diagnosis, and ongoing communication. You cannot conduct effective performance reviews or the supporting pieces without using essential communication skills effectively.

Oblivious to Communication Errors

Many people are completely oblivious to the communication errors they make. One manager had an open door policy, but when people visited him to talk out problems, he rarely looked up as they entered, answered in grunts and monosyllables, and was generally unreceptive. He ended up exeedingly frustrated when employees stopped trying and began to leave him out of the loop.

Good communication between manager and employee can make up for even the most grievous faults in a performance review system. Poor communication guarantees poor performance reviews. But even more importantly, poor communication creates the problems that make performance reviews seem painful. When a manager communicates poorly (generally throughout the year as well as during the performance review process), some or even all of the following consequences are:

- Employees become hesitant to work *with* their manager.
- Employees argue and reject their manager's input and opinions.
- Employees file more grievances related to performance issues.
- Employees don't keep their manager informed and avoid talking to their manager.
- Employees do their best to hide their deficiencies or performance difficulties.
- Employees refuse to take any responsibility.

There are other negative outcomes of poor communication. Even if we look at just the ones above, a little thought will tell you that these consequences aren't just abstract. They have concrete, specific, and quantifiable effects on the use of resources, efficiency and productivity, time (yours and others'), and work climate. All of these can be linked to your work unit's bottom line. So, when we talk about communication skills, we're *not* talking about "being nice" or "being a better human being." We're talking about skills that are closely tied to your ability to do your job and skills that are absolutely essential to the performance review process.

We're going to look at two families of communication skills. The first is the group of skills that you apply when you're telling and speaking—that is, when you have messages to send. The second is the

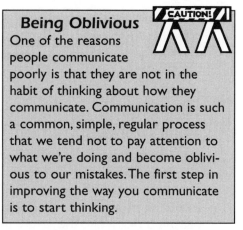

Being Oblivious
One of the reasons people communicate poorly is that they are not in the habit of thinking about how they communicate. Communication is such a common, simple, regular process that we tend not to pay attention to what we're doing and become oblivious to our mistakes. The first step in improving the way you communicate is to start thinking.

group of skills involved in how you react and respond to an employee and what he or she says. We're going to look at these two families with respect to the performance review meeting, but also as tools to use in performance planning, communicating throughout the year, and problem diagnostics. Before we discuss specific skills, let's look at some important facts about communication.

Communication Facts and Principles

Here are a few communication facts with which you may or may not be familiar. Use this list to remind yourself to *think* about how you communicate and prevent yourself from taking for granted the way you communicate.

- There's a difference between simply conveying information and communicating. Communication occurs only once the other person has heard, listened to, paid attention to, and understood the message you've tried to convey in the way you intended. Your communication job is to maximize the chances the person will get the meaning you intended.
- You can't completely control what the other person will get from what you say or write. But you can and should communicate in such a way that it's more *likely* that

common understanding will result and you'll catch misunderstandings early.

- We know that there are certain ways of communicating that make it almost impossible for the other person to receive what you have to send. Poor tone of voice, poor body language, and poor choice of words and phrases can virtually guarantee that the other person will not listen and may fight or otherwise resist or reject out of hand what you say.

- Contrary to common belief, communication doesn't occur sequentially. That is, both parties send and receive *at the same time*. While they may take turns sending and appear to take turns receiving, they also receive while they're sending. That means that how you behave while the other person is speaking is important in determining whether the communication process works.

- We tend to believe that our communication responsibilities involve primarily what *we* say. That's not complete. We also are responsible for creating an atmosphere that makes it easier for the other person to say what he or she has to say. In other words, we need to use our communication skills to create dialogue, where both people are active participants. That's particularly important when there's an imbalance of formal power, such as between an employee and his or her boss, which is the case with performance-related discussions.

Generative Skills

Don't be thrown off by the unfamiliar term in this heading. Generative communication skills determine your ability to send (or generate) messages so the other person can hear, listen, and understand them. So, when you offer an opinion, that's generative. When you greet a person, that's generative. When you write a narrative about a person's performance successes, that's generative.

How You Say What You Want to Say

A conversation is much more complicated than we generally realize. There's a lot that goes on. There are the words used, the tone of voice conveying those words, the meanings of those words for each of the participants, the associations of those words for each of the participants,

> ### Sending Information Isn't Communicating
>
> **⚠ CAUTION!**
>
> Do not mistake talking or sending information for communicating. Communication is about creating common understanding and exchanging meaning. Communication isn't complete until the other person understands what you say in the way that you mean it. Don't simply assume that the other person is hearing your words as you intend.

and the effects of body language. These factors influence how well the parties communicate and understand each other and the degree to which they are open to each other's messages. It's fair to say that conversations are like the proverbial icebergs— 90% below the surface. In practical, real-life terms, it's easy to make conversational errors that completely turn off the other person or create bad feelings and resentment. Even the best communicators do that sometimes. Even the kindest and best-intentioned people do that sometimes.

In the performance review process, so much is based on how things are said that you need to pay special attention to make sure you're not unnecessarily causing communication problems, particularly when the topics can be sensitive. Discussions about performance *can* be sensitive, so you're more likely to cause damage by how you say what you want to say.

We know there are a number of factors that create resistance and aggression in conversations. It's very important that you do *not* make these common mistakes in any of your interactions with employees, but particularly during performance-related discussions. Let's look at these "fire starters."

Lack of Listening and Understanding. When you do not listen and do not prove to the other person that you're trying to understand and demonstrate that you *do* understand, the other person pulls back and resists or rejects what you say. When you stop listening and trying to understand, so does the other person. We'll talk about listening skills in more detail later in the chapter.

"Less than" Communication. This term refers to anything you might say that implies that the other person is "less than" you or somehow below you in skill, ability, dedication, and so on. This applies more to comments about the person, rather than his or her behavior. You can talk about performance dropping off or other concrete, factual observations, but if you suggest the other person is "less than" or somehow faulty *as a person*, constructive communication will stop and destructive communication begins. Be alert to indirect implications. Take the following statement. "If you were really a loyal employee, you would work the overtime we are asking you to put in." That statement implies that the employee is *not* loyal and puts the employee in a "less than" position. You need to eliminate those kinds of statements.

Communicating Mistrust. Anything you say that suggests that you have no faith in the employee is problematic. Here's an example. Let's say that, during a performance review meeting, Frank, the employee, promises to take steps to complete his work tasks on time. The manager replies, "Frank, just to make sure, you *will* get these upcoming projects finished on schedule?" By asking this question after the employee has made his promise, the manager is telling the employee that he doesn't really believe him. That's not what the words actually say, but it *is* what Frank is going to get from the question, even if that's not the manager's intent. This is a good example of the communication iceberg.

Violation of Conversational Rules. This one is easy. Conversations have rules. In civil conversations, there are expectations. It's expected you won't interrupt. It's expected that you will link what you say to what the other person has said, rather than abruptly change the subject. It's expected that when you ask a question, you'll wait long enough for the person to answer and not answer it yourself. When you violate those conventions, you show "conversational bad faith"—and conflict usually results.

Blatant Generalizations and Exaggerations. Comments like "You never get your work done on time" or "You always seem to be in the middle of arguments with your colleagues" are examples of blatant generalizations. Not only are these kinds of statements inaccurate, since nobody is *always* or *never* doing anything, but also they tend to create resistance in the other person. Commit to accuracy and precision in what you say and don't generalize for dramatic effect.

Power-Based or Status-Based Comments. Nobody likes to feel pushed around, threatened, or coerced. While you may get an employee to comply with your wishes by threatening or pulling rank, you're not likely to get his or her cooperation by doing so. It's very difficult to succeed as a manager if all you have is compliance.

Here's an example of power-based talk: "I'm the manager around here and what I say goes." Here's an example of a status-based comment: "I've been doing this job a lot longer than you, so we're going to do it my way." Note also that this is a "less than" statement also by implication.

Now, we're *not* saying that you can never make decisions by virtue of your status or power as a manager. Sometimes you need to make unilateral decisions that an employee may dislike. But you want to make sure you're not flaunting your power or rubbing it in the face of the employee. You can make unilateral managerial decisions without sounding overbearing and aggressive.

There are some other ways in which how you say what you say can destroy meaningful and cooperative discussions during performance-related conversations. Take a look at the checklist in the sidebar, "Checklist of Destructive Language."

Checklist of Destructive Language

TOOLS Here are other factors that tend to create resistance and aggression in other people:

- Provide unsolicited advice. (See the section on feedback.)
- Appear to be trying to make someone feel guilty.
- Offer false or unrealistic assurances.
- Make fake or unrealistic positive comments (e.g., "It will be all right" when it clearly won't be).
- Appear to want to blame rather than fix.
- Appear to want to *win* the discussion rather than find a solution.
- Come across as infallible.
- Use excessively dramatic or histrionic language and behavior.
- Use hot words and phrases (words like "stupid," "dumb," and "incompetent").

Feedback Skills

The performance review meeting is a forum for accomplishing a great many things, but one of the most important is to provide some form of feedback to the employee about his or her performance. There's a huge body of research that tells us that high-quality feedback is essential for fast performance improvements.

Before we talk about how to deliver feedback effectively, we need to distinguish between feedback and judgment or evaluation. Evaluation is assessing or judging someone's contributions. Feedback is providing information, from your point of view, about what you've seen and heard. The feedback process needs to focus on improving performance by making information available to the employee. There's an additional function for feedback, to send a message that the employee's work is appreciated. Admittedly the line between feedback and judgment gets blurry. However, we still need to make the distinction so we avoid making judgmental verbal attacks on employees that we try to justify by calling our comments "feedback."

We'll walk through the characteristics of good feedback, but here's your guiding principle. If what you say is truly aimed at improving performance and it contains enough information to start the improvement process, then you're probably on the right track. If, however, part of what you say or want to say would be absolutely useless in terms of helping someone improve, you're not providing feedback anymore. For example, if you say, "Your performance has been horrible," that's not feedback. That's a pointless statement that the employee will perceive as an attack and reject. If you say, "I've noticed your sales figures are down, and I think that might be because ...," that's useful—that's feedback.

If you think feedback is important *only* during the performance review meeting, think again. In fact, you'll get the most mileage out of it when you use it all year, as you communicate with your employees in formal or informal ways.

So, here's how to provide feedback that works.

Be Supportive. Feedback is best heard and received when it is offered in a nonthreatening and encouraging way. That means you need a certain degree of emotional neutrality and calmness when you deliver feedback. Feedback that is encouraging doesn't focus just on the past but is forward-looking and clearly aimed at helping your employees improve in the future.

Be Direct. When we feel uncomfortable about saying something that might be a bit negative, we tend to hesitate or beat around

> **Ask for Feedback**
>
> Here's something that should not surprise you. When you're willing to listen to feedback from employees about *your* work, your employees will be much more willing to listen to the feedback you provide on *their* work. So ask. Make it standard in performance reviews to get feedback as well as give it.
>
> **Smart Managing**

the bush or hint. That's not good. In offering feedback, it's good to be as direct as possible. That doesn't mean being blunt or rude, but it does mean eliminating things like innuendo or hinting. Being direct also means that you make it clear *why* you're offering this specific feedback. Be careful not to offer a bogus reason. If you say your purpose is to help the employee improve, and then you attack or insult him or her, you're going to destroy any credibility you have.

Be Specific. Feedback works best when it is specific and includes concrete references to particular events. Saying, "You don't handle your customer calls quickly enough" is too vague to be useful. Try to reference a specific call or observation. That's why it's good to take notes to keep track of any particular situations you may want to discuss with employees. You can use those notes to refresh your memory of specifics of a particular event.

Describe Behavior. Focus feedback on what a person does and what is under the control of the person and keep away from personality, "attitude," or other aspects that are generally not under the control of the person. If you feel there's an attitude issue, reference it by talking about behaviors or indicators of the attitude, rather than the attitude itself.

Avoid Micromanaging

Be alert to the possibility that you're monitoring employees and providing feedback to such an extent that you're meddling, micromanaging. Employees need space to do their jobs and you need to be able to trust them enough to do those jobs without constant monitoring.

Don't Overwhelm. People can assimilate only a certain amount of information before getting overwhelmed. An employee who is overwhelmed by the sheer volume of the feedback you're providing is going to shut down. In performance reviews, you don't necessarily have to discuss every little thing. Also, here's where it's so important to have ongoing communication. If you can provide good feedback throughout the year, you won't need to dump a whole lot of feedback on the employee during the performance review.

Consider Timing. There are times when a person is open to feedback and times when a person is not. For example, if an employee is angry, tired, hungry, or stressed, it's probably not the right time to begin a feedback process. This caution also applies to you. If you are stressed, angry, or tired and try to deliver feedback, you are more likely to misspeak or make errors.

Share Control. Feedback works best when the other person has consented to participate or has requested it. Otherwise it's just "unsolicited advice"—and we all know how that usually comes across. Here's a simple way to do it. "Joe, I'd like to talk a bit about some things I've noticed about how you handle some phone calls. Can we do that?" Also feedback works best when it's part of a dialogue. Don't ramble on. Give a little feedback. Then ask the person whether that makes sense to him or her. Explore that issue interactively before moving on to something else. You don't need to be subservient or provide only the feedback the employee wants. Sometimes there are things that you need to deal with, whether an employee has asked for feedback or not. The key is not to become overbearing or overcontrolling in the feedback process.

Joint Action Plan. In giving feedback, managers tend to focus on what employees need to do to improve. To support the perception that you're providing feedback to improve performance, it's good to

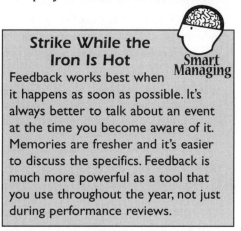

Strike While the Iron Is Hot

Smart Managing

Feedback works best when it happens as soon as possible. It's always better to talk about an event at the time you become aware of it. Memories are fresher and it's easier to discuss the specifics. Feedback is much more powerful as a tool that you use throughout the year, not just during performance reviews.

end a feedback session with a joint action plan to deal with what's been discussed and map out what the employee has agreed to do *and* what you have agreed to do. Don't dump everything on the employee. Participate actively in the solution.

Confirm. One common mistake that managers make with feedback is to believe their perception is 100% accurate. Keep in mind that your observations may be inaccurate and that, in any case, you need to confirm or discuss your observations and get the employee's perceptions on the table too. Managers can be wrong, you know!

What You Write and How You Write It

Performance management and review systems, because they tend to be driven by human resources departments staff who want to have documented paper trails, can push managers into believing that what's written down is much more important than what's discussed face to face. By now you understand that the verbal communication during reviews is far more important. However, that's not to discount the importance of what you write when documenting performance review conversations, and how you communicate with employees in writing.

Where does the written word fit? First, it's used to generate documentation or summaries of performance-related discussions, agreements, and decisions. Second, some managers use the written word to communicate to employees about how to prepare for performance related meetings—memos, really.

We're going to focus here on writing documentation. Since we've already explained the documentation process and what should be included in Chapter 4, let's concentrate on the actual process of writing.

First, let's look at what you write down. You need to have enough written down to satisfy the following conditions:

- Both you and the employee must be able to read it and understand what it means. What you write down must be detailed enough so it can jog memories as much as a year or two after you write it.
- There must be enough information so that a third party can make sense out of it in the event of any dispute or allegation about the accuracy and fairness of any decisions based on the discussions or decisions the documentation is meant to record.

On the other hand, there's a major downside to writing too much. The more you write, the less clear the documentation gets, because the most critical points tend to get lost in a sea of less important things and unnecessary words. Imagine looking at two very important trees in front of you. You can see them both very clearly. Now imagine those trees are surrounded by hundreds of other trees. Those very important trees become almost invisible. You can't see the trees for the forest. It's the same with words. Write down what's absolutely necessary, but no more.

How much is enough? There's no one right answer to that question. You have to use your judgment. But since the employee has to review and understand what you write down, you can use him or her as a good barometer. Ask, "Is this clear to you?" and "Do you think there's enough information here so that someone might be able to understand exactly what we are trying to say?"

The same caution applies to any other written communication you have with employees. In all written communication, you sacrifice clarity when you write too little or too much.

Whatever you have to put into writing is important, but how you write it is going to affect the reader's perceptions of your state of mind, your attitude, your intent, your motivation, and your credibility—and those perceptions *are* going to affect an employee's willingness to work with you in the performance management and review process. No matter what you're writing, follow these guidelines.

Collaborative Writing

Smart Managing

Final documents should be based on a collaboration between manager and employee. Encourage the employee to contribute to the wording and accuracy of what is written. Once something is on paper, allow some time for the employee to review, revise, and alter it before you finalize it into the document that you both sign.

Write for Clarity. That means using simple sentences and bullet formats where possible, staying on point, and organizing your thoughts before writing a word. One common error is to write without organizing first. That results in a kind of hodgepodge of words in which it's hard to discern the main points.

For example, if you're writing a critical incident report or a narrative as a way of documenting good or poor performance, start by identifying the one or two key points you need to communicate. Then use those points to organize into paragraphs. In the first paragraph, state the main point in the first sentence and then, to support that point, describe what you saw or heard. Then do the same for your next main point in another paragraph.

Also keep in mind that when you write down performance-related information, your goal is not to impress and not even to convince, but just to *describe*. That will help you improve the clarity of your writing.

Eliminate Hyperbole and Highly Charged Emotional Statements. Your written records need to reflect that you're being both fair and accurate in your observations about an employee. When you exaggerate or use words that are emotionally charged, you risk destroying any perception of fairness. If and when a third party reviews your written records, he or she will quickly assume, from the wording, that you are likely biased and even perhaps "out to get" an employee, even if that's not the case. Of course, when you exaggerate or use highly charged statements, you're almost guaranteed to create disagreement and strong resistance from employees.

Managers tend to exaggerate and use emotional language when they make general evaluative statements about an employee or a situation. That's another good reason to be specific. Let's take an example. You write, "The way Mary handled that customer was the worst instance of customer service I've ever seen." Is it really the worst? Or is this an exaggeration for effect? Whether it's accurate or not, it's going to sound like an exaggeration and it puts you in a bad light. Is it emotionally

charged? You bet! If Mary reads this, is she going to say to herself, "Well, golly, I'm glad my boss wrote that because it really
helps"? Or is she more likely to react like this? "Why is this person attacking me?"

Avoid Inferences. An inference is a conclusion you draw about
something you cannot observe *directly*. For example, when you
comment on someone's motivation, intent, ability, and so on,
you're drawing an inference. Those things are not directly
observable. Inferences are as much a reflection on you, in making the inferences, as they are on the employee.

Here's an example. "Mary continues to demonstrate a horrible attitude toward her job." That's an inference. It's "fightin'
words" guaranteed to destroy any possibility of working with
Mary and it makes you look bad to people who might read the
document. Here's the way to avoid inferences: stick to behavior.
Describe what you observe in Mary's behavior that points to a
"horrible attitude" and completely avoid mentioning "attitude."
For example: "Mary's absenteeism is about double that of her
colleagues, and she has been late for at least three important
customer meetings in the last month." Another example: "Mary
has been involved in two arguments with colleagues that have
required managerial intervention."

Responding and Eliciting Skills

So far, we've focused mostly on what *you* say, orally or in writing, and how *you* say it. While all of that is important, there's a
set of communication skills that are much more critical in making the performance management and review process work.
They're much more critical because of the point we made at the
start of this book: performance reviews can be valuable only
when they're conducted within a spirit of partnership, shared
ownership, and dialogue. That means that however important it
is for you to talk, offer feedback, and so on, it's as important or
even more important to involve the employee in the discussion
as an active, contributing partner. Some employees will natural-

TRICKS OF THE TRADE

Accommodating Differences

Some employees jump in. Some you can encourage to jump in. Some are shy or simply not comfortable in certain kinds of discussions. You need to be flexible here. You want participation but you can't *force* it. Your job is to open the door to participation, rather than pushing the employee through the door. Be patient. It can take a long time to get to the trust point where shy people will open up.

ly participate actively with little or no encouragement, if you give them the chance. Many other employees need to be encouraged to do so. That's where this set of skills is critical.

Responding and eliciting skills are what make you more able to use ways of communicating that both demonstrate that you're listening to the input of the employee and taking it seriously and directly draw employees into the discussion. Both are important.

It's likely you're at least somewhat familiar with these skills. Please keep in mind that the purpose of using these techniques is not to appear "nice" or for some other vague, touchy-feely reason. Responding and eliciting skills are essential to achieving a number of specific concrete outcomes that eventually impact on productivity and bottom-line results.

Questioning Skills

Questioning is your most powerful tool to get employees to talk, contribute, and interact with you during the review meeting and, for that matter, during any of the components of the larger performance management process. Let's start with a few basic issues.

Questions are important. There are two factors that will determine whether you'll succeed in using them to involve employees.

First, no amount of questioning skill can compensate for a situation where employees distrust you. Where there is a lack of trust, employees will respond minimally, offering little and keeping information and their own perceptions to themselves. That means that it will be almost impossible to do proper problem

---

A Trust Checklist

Employees tend to trust managers who:
- Share information and explain decisions
- Do what they say they're going to do
- Act consistently in predictable ways
- Work on behalf of the employees in addition to working on behalf of the organization
- Trust and have faith in their employees
- Show an interest in employees as human beings

---

diagnosis or improve things. Trust in the workplace is a complicated issue, but here's what you need to remember. The degree to which employees trust you depends on your words and actions throughout the entire year. You must nurture that trust in everything you do. Also, it may not be possible to create bonds of trust with every employee. Employees decide whom to trust and whom not to trust—and sometimes those decisions aren't entirely rational.

Second, you can ask all the questions you want and phrase them just perfectly, but if you don't respond properly to what employees say, employees will simply stop participating. Employees will work with you and discuss things openly, provided they believe that you're genuinely interested in what they say and that you aren't asking questions just for show. Some managers tend to ask questions to try to appear interested, when in fact they've already made their decisions or they have no intention of listening or giving credence to what the employee says. Employees are really smart: they figure this out very quickly. If they conclude this is the case, they'll write you off. So, while we can talk about questioning as a way of eliciting responses and involvement, don't forget that how you respond to what they say is at least as important.

Open-Ended Versus Closed-Ended Questions. There are two basic kinds of questions: open-ended and closed-ended. Each has its place in performance-related discussions.

Open-ended questions are those that leave a lot of room for

the respondent to answer in ways that she or he sees fit. For example, "How do you feel about the meeting?" is open-ended. "How do you feel things have gone in the last year?" is open-ended.

Closed-ended questions are those that usually elicit a short and very specific answer. For example, "Which of the following best describes your feelings about the meeting—comfortable or uncomfortable?" is closed, because it asks for a single, con-strained, one-word answer. Questions that ask for a yes or no answer, for a choice between or among options (like the above example), or for a specific detail (such as "When did that hap-pen?" or "How many meetings did you miss?") tend to be closed-ended.

There's nothing inherently better about one kind of question or another. Both have uses.

Open-ended questions are much better for involving employees in discussions and getting less structured responses and probably more infor-mation. Open-ended ques-tions usually get you longer responses, but the responses may veer off topic or ramble. On the other hand, open-ended questions get you more information, with the potential for more nuggets of important information.

When Things Start Wandering

If an employee starts wandering on tangents, you can refocus using clarifying questions. For example, "John, I'm not clear about how what you said relates to the issue of cus-tomer complaints. Could you explain the link a bit more?"

These are particularly useful when trying to diagnose the source of performance barriers. Open-ended questions work best to get employees talking and when both parties are calm and relative-ly unemotional. When emotions run high, responses to open-ended questions will go "all over the block."

Closed-ended questions fit well in situations where you need to exert a bit more control over the discussion—in situations where emotions run high. They are also really excellent in beginning a process of creating agreements on small points to start building bridges of cooperation. This is a common negotiating tactic. Get agreement on a few small points to create a basis of goodwill. Closed-ended questions are also good for summarizing decisions or the gist of discussions. For example, "OK, John, so we've talked about a few things that you can do to achieve the goals you need to hit to receive a pay raise. They are ... (details). Is that your understanding?"

Clearly you're going to use a mix of open and closed questions. There are no hard-and-fast rules here, except to keep in mind that overuse of closed-ended questions may make you appear to be overly controlling and not really interested in the employee's input.

Clarifying Questions. Clarifying questions are really follow-up questions. They are used to ask the employee to expand on what he or she said, add to it, or explain further. These are very important. People tend to ask a single question, half-listen to the answer, and then take over the floor. That doesn't work in life—and it doesn't work in the performance review process. Here's an example of follow-up.

Manager: John, what do you think has contributed to your lower sales figures this quarter?

John: Oh, there are a lot of factors. The economy is really slow these days, and people just aren't spending the money. I'm also overworked with paperwork, and .... (He provides a few other answers.)

Manager: OK, John, let's go through them one by one. Which of the ones you mentioned seems to be the

> **⚠ CAUTION!**
>
> ### Don't Ignore Responses
>
> If you ask questions, you *must* demonstrate that you're paying attention to the answers you receive. When you ask a question and get a response, don't go into a monologue or move straight to the next question as if you're reading from a script. Use follow-up questions to demonstrate that you're interested and you want the discussion to be open.

biggest contributor to the lower sales?

The manager begins with an open-ended question. John replies and then the manager uses a clarifying, follow-up question to move the conversation along to make it more specific. You can probably think of other follow-up questions that the manager might use as this conversation progresses.

Questioning Guidelines

Here are some important guidelines to help you use questioning more effectively.

Don't ask questions when you're not prepared to hear the answers. Sometimes people ask questions but are willing only to accept a specific answer they have in mind. For example, if you really have no interest in hearing that you're a poor manager, don't ask, "Do you think I'm a good or poor manager?" When you ask a question, you have to be willing to consider whatever responses you get and not overreact.

Questions that start with "Why" tend to make people feel defensive. It's just a quirk of our language. You can replace "why" questions with phrasing that tends not to cause that reaction. For example, rather than asking, "Why are you late so often?" try "Are there any particular things that are getting in the way of arriving at work on time?" Notice the difference in feel?

Don't use questions to say things indirectly. This is a technique commonly used by parents on children and so it's interpreted as manipulative and patronizing. For example, "Don't you think you should be more diligent in completing your work?" isn't really a legitimate question. It's a rhetorical question—a statement dressed up as a question. It will be heard as "I want you to be more diligent in completing your work." Questions used to mask statements or requests create mistrust.

Avoid compound questions. A compound question consists of several parts: it's actually several questions in one. Compound questions are confusing and tend to result in low-quality responses. Here's an example: "Is there some reason why you have been late on many Fridays and why you tend to leave early on Wednesdays?" That's two questions and you're not likely to get good answers to both. Separate the issues and make your questions simpler and more specific.

Don't interrupt when a person is trying to answer a question you've posed. That's a general guideline; there are some exceptions. When the response is completely over the top, completely off the topic, insulting, or abusive, it's appropriate to interrupt and refocus. Do it gently. Try your best not to sound frustrated when refocusing.

Listening Skills

So far, we've focused on getting your employees to open up and share their knowledge and opinions within the context of performance reviews. As we said earlier, that's not the whole story. How you react to what an employee says is going to determine whether the discussion goes well and whether the employee continues to be an active, good-faith participant. There are two responding skill sets that encourage ongoing openness and participation. One involves your nonverbal responses; the other involves listening responses.

When we talk about listening, we're not just referring to your ability to hear what is said. What's more important is that you convey to the employee that you hear, understand, value, and are interested in what he or she has said. You have to *prove* to the person that you're hearing and understanding. That's where listening skills come in. As you'll see, listening skills are not only useful for creating an interactive climate in which you and the employee can work as

Use Active Listening to Make Sure

Keep in mind that misunderstandings occur more often than you might think and that they often remain undiscovered long enough to cause arguments and bad feelings. Active listening provides a tool for you to use to lessen misunderstandings—to verify that what you hear the person say is actually what the person meant.

partners, but also essential for avoiding misunderstandings and clarifying meaning.

Active listening, also known as reflective listening, refers to a process where you listen to what a person says, rephrase or summarize it, and send it back to the person for verification that what you understood is what he or she meant. It's really not complicated. Here's an example of reflective listening about a particular set of facts:

> So if I understand what you're saying, you're suggesting that one of the major problems interfering with (some job task) is that you're constantly being interrupted by other staff members asking you for advice. Have I got that right?

Here's a slightly different example where the focus is on an employee's feelings:

> John, I'm hearing that maybe you're a little frustrated with what you see as constantly changing directions on your projects. Is that true?

As you can see, you can use listening responses to clarify or to show interest in factual issues, but also to inquire about more emotional reactions, even when the employee has not brought up those emotions directly. That's not to say you *have* to delve into those more emotional reactions. You need to decide if they're relevant to the purpose of the meeting and your ability to maintain rapport with the employee and whether it's likely that exploring them will be fruitful.

Here are some listening tips.

- Don't overuse the technique. When you use it constantly, it interferes with the normal flow of conversation and starts to sound phony.
- Active listening should not come out like something that a social worker or a psychiatrist would say. Try not to sound "hip" or touchy-feely. That turns employees off.
- Listening responses need to be specific. "I hear you" and "I know where you're coming from" are not listening responses, because they don't prove to the speaker that

you actually do understand what he or she said. Stock statements like those are ineffective and sometimes provoke arguments. Don't use them.

- Listening responses need to be relatively short. Pick the major points and reflect those back to the employee in one or two relatively short sentences. It's not usually necessary to summarize everything that he or she has said.
- Don't ever, ever repeat verbatim what a person has said. Parroting only shows that you can "play back" what was said; it doesn't show whether you understood.
- Decouple the listening response from evaluation. Don't combine your listening responses with your opinions or judgments. Here's an example of what to avoid. "So, what I hear you saying is that ... (paraphrase), but I'm afraid I have to disagree strongly." Tacking on an opinion completely eliminates the benefits you receive from using active listening.

Nonverbal Skills

The second set of responding skills has to do with your nonverbals. Not only do you want to verbally show your interest in what the other person is saying, but you want to make sure that you're conveying interest through your body language and that you're not sending negative, discouraging messages.

There are certain postures that send a positive message of your interest. They include leaning forward toward the speaker and making appropriate eye contact while the other person is speaking. Oddly enough, apart from these important ones, using body language to convey interest and attention is largely about eliminating actions and postures that tell someone you *don't* care. Many people send messages of dis-

> **⚠️ CAUTION!**
>
> **Pay Attention**
> We pay even less attention to what our bodies communicate than to how we say things. It's very easy to unintentionally send messages of disinterest or disagreement with our body language and completely derail the review discussion. Pay attention.

interest and/or inattention through their nonverbal behavior, even when they are paying attention and interested. So let's focus on the things you need to avoid.

Here's a list of some nonverbal behaviors that tend to indicate disinterest or send other negative messages.

- Don't slouch. Avoid other postures that might make you look less alert.
- Keep your arms and legs uncrossed and relaxed, to send the message that you're open.
- Don't fiddle with pens, rings, or other objects while the other person is talking.
- Don't write while the other person is talking, unless you explain why. You can take notes—provided you explain that's what you are doing.
- Don't let your eyes wander or look at your watch or a clock.
- Don't shake your head while the other person is speaking.
- Don't sigh and/or roll your eyes.

If you keep in mind that your goal is to invite the employee to be a partner in the review enterprise and if you pay attention to how you're communicating, you'll probably do well with the communication process. The biggest impediment to good communication in the review process is that managers (and, of course, employees) simply do not pay enough attention to how they communicate and the possible negative effects on the other person's willingness to be an active partner in the discussion.

Manager's Checklist for Chapter 9

❏ How you communicate during the year and during any performance-related meetings is going to determine whether the performance review process is going to be difficult and uncomfortable or a more relaxed and constructive process.

❏ We tend to take communication for granted and not think

enough about what we're saying and how we're saying it. So, an essential step in improving is to start thinking about how you communicate.

❏ When writing documentation, be specific, be concise, and write to describe. Involve the employee in determining final drafts.

❏ People often inadvertently send messages that damage the conversation. Work to eliminate destructive ways of communicating by understanding the ways you can damage performance-related discussions and by getting rid of "fire starters."

❏ Provide feedback that is clearly intended to help the other person and not to attack or demean the other person.

❏ Use questions liberally to involve the employee and use follow-up questions to clarify and show your interest in what the employee says.

The Rewards and Punishment Dilemma

No discussion of performance reviews can be complete without tackling the issue of how performance reviews affect and are affected by rewards and punishments in the workplace. In this chapter we're going to describe the biggest obstacle to making performance reviews work and we're also going to explain why it's almost impossible to eliminate that obstacle. The purpose of this chapter is to help you understand the limitations and problems associated with linking performance reviews to rewards and punishments. It may not be possible to completely eliminate problems associated with linking reviews with rewards and punishments, but if you're aware of the potential problems, you'll be in a much better position to anticipate them and reduce any negative impact.

Imagine a Perfect World

Take a moment to visualize a work environment that, from the manager's chair, would be ... well ... perfect. If we could change five things, just five things, we could create an almost ideal environment in which to manage. In this perfect world:

- There is a perfectly reliable, objective method of measuring employee performance and contributions to the company and a perfect way to assess the value of each employee.
- All of your employees are competent and fairly good at their jobs and perform well. There are no poor performers.
- Your employees aren't picky about their salaries, promotions, or other rewards. Those things aren't important to them.
- Your employees have no egos. They're never defensive, they're always open to hearing how they could improve, and they don't get offended if you tell them they could improve their performance.
- Your company doesn't care how much salary it pays out.

That's it. Five simple things we can fantasize about—even though we know that this imaginary world is beyond our grasp and probably will never exist.

Now, let's imagine how you might reward employees in this perfect world, using your perfectly reliable, objective method for measuring value. You would simply calculate the value of each employee and then increase his or her salary according to the results of this objective assessment. You could and probably would still work to improve performance continuously.

Since the company, you, and your employees aren't concerned much about salaries or rewards, this would go

> ### Understanding Review Limits
> **Smart Managing**
>
> Your best weapon in reducing the negative outcomes resulting from tying rewards to reviews is understanding the limits of the review system and acknowledging, both to yourself and your employees, that there is *no* perfectly objective and relevant way to measure performance flawlessly.

quite well and employees would work with you to appraise their performances. Since money is not a big concern in this world, the frequency and intensities of conflict about rewards are significantly reduced. Since employees are egoless, they don't get offended by negative comments about their performances. There's no reason to negotiate, argue, or anything of that sort. There's no reason to hide, lie, or deceive.

What we've done is create an imaginary world where employee and manager can be on the same side of the fence in terms of the allocation of rewards. There's no fundamental conflict of interest between manager and employee. If you have trouble creating a vision of this world, you're normal. If you believe that it's impossible to have such a world, you're correct. But let's say it's there, and you're in it.

Within this strange world, you can determine rewards based on performance reviews *and* work *with* the employee to improve performance, based on those same performance reviews, because there are no inherent conflicts. The rewards are unimportant, employees don't become defensive or offended, and you have a perfect method for determining value.

Back to Our World

Let's step back into our world. First, we don't have a perfect or even nearly perfect way of assessing the value of an employee. We can guess, and that's what we try to do, but our ability to measure value and performance isn't even in the same universe as our ability to measure, say, body temperature or the distance between New York City and Pittsburgh. Second, employees care about salaries and promotions and rewards. Perhaps more importantly, they really, really care about fairness in compensation and rewards. If Joe thinks he's "better" than Mary and Mary is paid more, Joe gets really upset. Third, your company cares about how much it pays out in salaries, because the powers have it in their heads that staying in business is better than going bankrupt. Fourth, employees have egos and get defensive.

So what happens when you couple performance reviews to rewards? The reviews take on huge significance to everyone involved. Employees want every bit they can get and companies tend to want to minimize what they pay. It's a basic conflict. As soon as you tie reviews to pay or rewards, you create a situation where it's apparently not in the best interests of the employee or the manager to work together. Couple that conflict with the lack of good objective measures and the review process changes. A review process tied to rewards tends to pit manager vs. employee as each tries to maximize his or her benefits.

In this book we've said, over and over, that if performance reviews and performance management do not contribute to improving performance, they have no value or even take away value from the company. We've also said that the *only* way performance reviews can be used to improve performance is if employee and manager see each other on the same side, with similar interests. That's the problem.

The Rewards and Punishments Dilemma

This is a dilemma, because you have two choices and whichever one you choose will result in significant loss. It's the "between a rock and a hard place" phenomenon. If you link rewards and punishments to performance reviews, you set up a situation where the manager and employee are at cross-purposes. The manager wants to reward fairly, but has a limited pool of resources, while the employee wants fair compensation, but also wants to get as much as possible.

Placing the parties on different sides makes it very difficult to improve performance.

Punishment Isn't Just ...

Smart Managing

Good managers know that punishment isn't just doing something the employee doesn't want, but it also means withholding something the employee wants. Withholding a pay raise is usually seen as just as punishing as docking pay. Employees react based on *their* perceptions and managers need to anticipate negative reactions.

On the other hand, if you don't tie rewards and punishments to the performance review, you can develop and maintain a relationship where manager and employee are on the same side and have similar purposes—improving performance. However, that doesn't solve the problem of how to decide compensation or who gets promoted. If you don't use performance reviews to determine rewards, then what *do* you use?

In short, that's the dilemma: if you tie pay to reviews, you lose something important, but if you don't tie it to reviews, you have to have some other rational way of deciding pay levels. Either way you lose something important.

The Issue of Punishment

The rewards and punishments dilemma doesn't apply only to raises and promotions. In fact, the basic dilemma is far clearer when we talk about deciding on things that might be unpleasant for the employee. For lack of a better term, let's use the word "punishment" to describe actions like firing, laying off, suspending, or docking pay. In this context, "punishment" simply means something the employee doesn't like.

Key Term

Punishment Any actions that result in the employee losing something she or he already has and/or that deny something to the employee that she or he believes is due. Whether something is punishment or not is a matter of the employee's perceptions and is somewhat subjective.

Let's look at an example that highlights the difficulties of using performance reviews for improving performance *and* for making decisions that may negatively affect an employee.

Here are the players. Pat has 12 people reporting to him and by all accounts is a good manager, concerned about both the welfare and productivity of his staff. As is common, the employees don't really mistrust him, but they are aware that he has some power to make decisions that will affect their futures.

Jerry works for Pat. He's been with the company for about 10 years, working under Pat for the last two and a half years.

Jerry has never been a spectacular performer. Probably the most common adjective managers have used to describe his work is "average." He's not great, but not poor enough to warrant any formal action.

Over the last year, Pat has noticed gradual shifts in Jerry's at-work behavior and his productivity. There's been a general downturn. Absenteeism has increased. Customer complaints have increased slightly. Twice during the year, his coworkers have complained that Jerry has been obstructive in team meetings. Pat has some data that shows Jerry's production is down about 10% over the last year. That's not a lot, but taking all things together, Jerry is no longer doing the job at the level needed.

It's performance review time. At this company, review time is also the time that recommendations about salary raises, promotions, and demotions are made. To complicate the situation, the company's executives have made it known that line managers must be more rigorous and "hard-nosed" in making important staff decisions and cutting costs.

Pat's Performance Review Attempt

Put yourself in Pat's position. How would you approach the issue? What would you say in the initial review meeting? Here's how Pat approached the problem.

Pat: Jerry, we've talked about some of these things in the past year, but I'm a little concerned about the direction you have been moving in. What I'm seeing are some areas where you seem to be moving backwards. (Pat then talks about some of the data on absenteeism, production figures, and so on.)

I think we've had a pretty good working relationship over the years you've been here, so I'd like to see if we can work together to figure out what's causing these things and see if there's anything I can do to help bring your performance levels up to at least where they were two years ago, and perhaps even beyond that. To start off, I'd really like to get your input about the situation, so I have a few questions I'd like to ask you. First, do you agree that the things I outlined about your performance a minute ago are mostly accurate? (Jerry responds with something noncommittal, but grudgingly admits some of them.)

OK, well let's take a closer look at the productivity numbers, which seem fairly clear. According to this, yours is down 10%. Have you got any ideas why that's been the case?

Jerry: Well, you know, Pat, we got all this machinery in and I'm sure I'll get the hang of using it soon, but it's just taking me a long time. The drop in productivity is really small, and I'm sure things will be back to normal real soon.

Pat: Is there anything I can do to help you get in sync with the new stuff?

Jerry: I don't think so. I'm on top of it. Guaranteed things will get better in the next month.

Keeping in mind that we're looking at only a small portion of the entire conversation, what's your opinion about Pat's way of coming at this performance problem? It looks pretty good to me. He's attempted to open the door to work with Jerry, hasn't made any accusations or otherwise insulted Jerry, and is trying very hard to get Jerry's input. From this conversation, we also know that none of the issues are new to Jerry and that the two have discussed them a little during the year.

So, let's say we agree that Pat is handling this well. What's your opinion of how the meeting is going? That's a different story. It takes two to diagnose performance problems and develop solutions and, despite Pat's efforts, Jerry has not gushed forth a fountain of useful information. In fact Jerry is doing what many employees do—downplaying the significance of the problems and promising things will change. He's not being overtly difficult, but neither is he participating actively in a process that is intended to help him. Why?

From Where Jerry Sits

Here are some of the things Jerry knows and/or believes about this situation. We're going to distinguish between the two by putting a "K" beside what he knows and a "B" beside what he believes is true but might not be.

- Jerry knows that Pat has the power to reward or punish him and therefore affect his life on a broad scale, for example, whether he can feed his kids properly or make the mortgage payment. (K)
- Jerry realizes his performance has been dropping. (K)
- Jerry knows some of the reasons why his performance has been dropping. (K)
- Jerry knows the general situation in the company and the desire expressed by management to become leaner and meaner. (K)
- Jerry believes that, if push comes to shove, Pat will do what the executives tell him. (B)
- Jerry believes that Pat, even if he means well, is probably going to try to demote him, cut his salary, or put him on probation. (B)
- Jerry believes the best thing to do is gloss over the problem, hoping that by promising improvement and keeping the discussion short, he will prevent Pat from making any decisions that will negatively affect him. (B)

Given Jerry's perspective and what he knows, the things he believes are true (but may not be) are quite reasonable, in the absence of strong evidence to refute those beliefs.

Now, put yourself in Jerry's position. Given the above, do you really want to work with Pat to diagnose and solve the performance issues, when that process would require you to further expose and share things that might potentially portray you in a poor light? Let's not forget that it's a reasonable assumption that complete, open disclosure might lead to even worse consequences than are in view right now.

It's Perceptions That Count

Smart Managing Keep in mind that people behave according to their beliefs about the situation, and not some objective "truth." Commit to teasing out any perceptions and beliefs that may be causing the employee to be less cooperative than might be beneficial for both of you.

Let's add just a little more information into the equation—the reason Jerry's performance has dropped. Jerry is suffering from rheumatoid arthritis, which, he has been told, will get worse over time. The immediate symptoms include pain and joint stiffness; the latter makes it hard for him to learn the skills needed to operate the recently acquired equipment. The medications he is forced to take to deal with the symptoms tend to make him less alert and more irritable, so he has problems with coworkers. His real concern is that, if he reveals all this to Pat, he will definitely be demoted or let go, which could mean the end of his career in his current profession. So, while revealing the problem might help forestall any immediate punishments, he worries that management will use knowledge of his physical condition as a basis to get rid of him.

Jerry may have it all wrong, but he believes, because Pat has the power to reward or to punish, that if he's honest he will lose more than if he plays down the issue, tries to fake his way past it, and hopes some medications will be found that will eliminate the cause. If that happens, whose fault is it? It doesn't matter since the problem becomes the manager's problem.

The Fairness Challenge

There's yet another issue involved here, with respect to Pat and Jerry—fairness. Pat has an obligation to make decisions about rewards and punishments. Since Jerry hasn't revealed the underlying reasons for the lower performance, it probably will make sense to Pat to withhold the usual annual pay raise until Jerry comes up to the appropriate performance levels.

Let's assume that's what happens. Is it fair to penalize Jerry for something that's really beyond his control? There's no easy

> ## Avoid Creating Performance Problems
>
> **CAUTION!**
>
> How you act when small performance problems occur is going to determine whether you fix those problems or create huge, long-term, irresolvable problems. Actions that are perceived as unfair or punitive are likely to increase problems, not fix them. Small problems require small, cooperative solutions so they don't become big ones.

answer to that question; good people may, in good faith, come down on different sides. So, let's ask another question. If Pat penalizes Jerry (either knowing or not knowing the underlying cause of the performance problem), how is that likely to affect Jerry's attitudes and future performance? We can't say with certainty, but many employees will perceive such action as unfair and respond accordingly. In other words, withholding a pay raise in this situation may not spur Jerry on to greater performance; in fact, it may contribute to a performance slide that is permanent and irreversible.

This kind of reaction may seem exceedingly illogical to you. How can Jerry think it's unfair for Pat to withhold a raise when he himself isn't providing the information that might convince Pat that such a "punishment" isn't appropriate? It is illogical. Unfortunately, people aren't always logical and rational.

Summarizing the Problem

So, let's sum up the dilemma. If you tie pay (or other rewards and punishments) to performance reviews, it tends to place employee and manager in adversarial positions, which interferes with problem-solving and improving performance. If you don't tie pay to performance reviews, you have no obvious way of rewarding good and exceptional performance.

Addressing the Dilemma

You can't eliminate the dilemma. What you can do is reduce the negative impact of this fact of life. Let's look at a few important issues.

The Trust Solution

What's interesting about this dilemma is that when there's a strong relationship of trust between manager and employee, the effects of this dilemma virtually disappear. When and if the employee believes the manager has the employee's best interests at heart and the manager has demonstrated a willingness to work cooperatively with the employee, the employee becomes much more open and forthcoming *even* if he or she understands that the manager can affect his or her compensation. The large majority of employees are reasonable human beings and can deal with difficult realities—provided they believe in the honesty and loyalty of the manager. Employees understand. In an atmosphere of trust, they can even accept that bad things sometimes happen and they won't necessarily take "punishments" as comments about them as human beings. Employees even recognize and accept that managers don't have free rein but also need to operate in accordance with their marching orders.

Where there is distrust between manager and employee, all bets are off. The employee will fight against any "punishments," even when he or she realizes these are probably deserved. The greater the mistrust, the more he or she will fight.

Of course, the task of creating trust and rapport with staff

Trust Factors

Here are some factors that increase employee trust of managers:

- Openness and transparency (all agendas are on the table)
- Honesty
- Walking the talk
- Consistency in action and words
- Demonstrated commitment (through actions) to helping the employee succeed
- Demonstrated commitment (through listening) to understand the employee
- Moderate, limited use of power to solve problems

doesn't start during the performance review. In fact, you need to address the trust issue in everything you do, since the employees judge and trust or distrust according to what they see you do and say all year long. If you create that sense of trust throughout the year, you will find that even when you and an employee disagree during the performance review discussion, that trust will carry you past the rough spots.

Focusing on Agreement, Not Objectivity

If you want a nuts-and-bolts strategy to minimize the effects of the rewards dilemma, look to the performance planning process. Reward dilemma problems are magnified when clear reward criteria are lacking. If you and the employee have not established what the employee needed to accomplish to be rewarded (or to avoid perceived punishment), then you are at high risk during and after the performance review meeting when you communicate decisions about those rewards to the employee.

That's why it's so important to establish a shared understanding of the performance/reward criteria during the performance planning phase (see Chapter 6). We want the criteria to be as clear, measurable, and objective as possible. That said, you need to know that it's very difficult to establish clear, unambiguous criteria in a meaningful way. It's easy to be objective and to measure trivial work behavior, but that work behavior is probably not a fair measure of the employee's value. It's much more difficult to measure what's really important and it's difficult to measure an employee's total and complete contribution.

So, during the performance planning process, you should focus on creating and agreeing upon a set of criteria without

Avoid the Low-Hanging Fruit

Don't be seduced into setting performance/reward criteria on the basis of how measurable they are, since the most easily measurable parts of job performance are also often the least meaningful in determining an employee's value or contributions. You can't totally eliminate subjectivity and ambiguity.

focusing only on the criteria that are easy to measure. If you focus on getting agreement about performance/reward criteria, it will be far easier to apply those criteria to determine rewards. This applies regardless of whether the performance review system supplied to you by your company requires you to create these expectations upfront or not. Do it!

When you have good rapport with your employees, a sense of trust, *and* reasonably clear, agreed-upon criteria, you will go a long way to eliminating the negative effects of the "rewards dilemma."

Future Focus

One of the criticisms leveled at the performance review process is that it's like driving a car while looking in the rearview mirror. In other words, it involves looking backwards to events and circumstances now etched in the stone of history. You can't change them. The perspectives of looking backward and looking forward affect employee attitudes differently within the context of rewards and punishment.

Let's say that at the conclusion of the performance review meeting, you address the issue of whether John is going to receive a pay increase based on his performance during the past year. Since the economy has been soft, the pool available for raises is small and only the top performers are going to receive raises. John, while above average, is not yet a top performer. Less skilled managers, even though they may convey the bad news to John as gently as possible, forget to focus on the future. They might explain the fiscal situation, the soft economy, express their regret, and use other important interpersonal skills to soften the blow.

Let's contrast this with how the expert manager deals with this situation.

> **CAUTION!**
>
> **Promises You Can Keep**
> Focusing on the future involves some uncertainty. Make sure that if you offer incentives for future performance you can deliver. It's a good idea to consult with your superiors or HR to find out what you can promise.

She might use those very same skills as the less skilled managers, but the difference is that she focuses the employee on what he or she needs to do to receive a raise the next time. In effect she is saying, "We can't increase your pay right now, but we can revisit this in three months, and if you have achieved X, Y, and Z, I think we can do something." While the lesser manager focuses on what's past and offers no hope of any change in the future, the more expert manager provides an incentive to the employee that is attainable and possible in the foreseeable future. That has a huge effect on the employee's perceptions and the motivation to achieve. Clearly the desire to receive the offered incentive is likely to fuel the employee's productivity. But equally important is that the employee is more likely to see the manager as helpful and trying to work with the employee and act in the best interests of the employee, to the degree that is possible.

Changing Compensation Modes

The final possibility we can suggest to address the rewards dilemma is to examine whether it's possible to change the compensation system. Many of us are not in control of how salaries are determined or how rewards are administered, particularly in larger corporations or government organizations. While you may not be in ultimate and total control of reward methods, that's not to say it isn't worth investigating whether you can encourage those who *are* in control of those resources to allocate even a small additional percentage to the reward pool or to consider other methods to decide on pay bonuses, besides linking them to performance reviews.

One of the most promising methods is to continue to reward based on individual merit and to supplement that with benefits when and if the work unit or company has a good year. That can be done in several different ways. A percentage of net profits can be distributed evenly throughout the company or a fixed percentage of net profits (or sales) can be allocated as the reward pool, to allow both a minimum salary increase for everyone *and* a merit increase range.

Altering the compensation system doesn't get rid of the rewards dilemma—nothing does completely; the idea may fit your work environment or it may not. Compensation in and of itself is an exceedingly complex issue, beyond the scope of this book. We offer this alternative as something you might want to explore.

Summing Up

Since we don't work in a perfect world, we need to be aware of the effects of the rewards dilemma and try to reduce negative impacts that come from the obligation to pay and reward employees. It's doubtful that you can ever eliminate all the negative effects possible with respect to every single person in your employ.

So, what's the bottom line? When the employee trusts the manager and the manager takes a forward-looking approach to the rewards issue, the negative effects are significantly reduced. Will this eliminate grumbling, bad attitudes, and disappointment for every single employee? No, of course not. We're dealing with people here; even if you do everything absolutely perfectly, someone is going to end up upset at some point.

As a final comment, we've focused on tangible rewards in this chapter—promotions, salaries, bonuses, and so on, because the concrete rewards-reviews dilemma involves concrete tangible rewards. Please don't think that we believe the only thing that drives performance is these concrete rewards. We don't. There are many other, intangible rewards—such as recognition of a job well done, awards, opportunities to development new skills, new job responsibilities, and so on—that can affect performance in significant ways.

Manager's Checklist for Chapter 10

❏ All managers must face the fact that tying pay raises and other rewards to performance reviews may be both necessary and likely to create friction and problems for the performance review process.

❏ You can't eliminate the conflict inherent in tying perform-ance reviews to rewards. What you can do is be aware of that inherent conflict and work toward reducing its nega-tive consequences.

❏ Consciously creating a relationship of trust between you and each employee is probably the best way to address the rewards dilemma. Do it!

❏ When denying rewards or raises, do your best to set the bar for the future, to provide realistic achievable incentives *for the future.*

❏ Set those future-oriented bars so employees can reach them and you and each employee can evaluate his or her progress as soon as possible. Re-evaluation in three months, for example, is better than waiting until a full year has passed.

Reviews with Employees of Different Stripes

Employees aren't all alike. Some are excellent performers, some are about average, and some perform at lower levels. Employees also differ within each of these groups. For example, in the "lower performance" category, some employees are eager to learn but haven't yet "arrived," while some perform poorly and show little interest in working with you to improve performance.

There are other differences too. Some employees function best when you deal with them in very firm ways, while other employees don't react positively to firmness and need more gentle guidance.

It doesn't make sense for performance reviews to be identical across the board. While it's important that you treat employees fairly and in equivalent ways, that doesn't mean you have to treat employees exactly the same. How you conduct review meetings depends on the employee's specific situation and your own "best guess" as to what tone will work best with each specific employee. For example:

- Employee A performs poorly due to lack of experience but wants to learn.
- Employee B performs poorly and resists feedback and suggestions.
- Employee C performs poorly and just doesn't care.
- Employee D excels and is comfortable where he is.
- Employee E excels and is ambitious and eager for new challenges.

Can you think of ways you might conduct performance reviews differently for the poor performer who wants to learn and with the employee who just doesn't care? Sure! In the first instance, you might be far more patient and supportive; in the latter, you might begin a disciplinary process. How about the two employees who excel? You might consider grooming the excellent and ambitious employee for more advanced duties, while you may be more concerned with maintaining the performance levels of the excellent but unambitious employee.

In this chapter we're going to look at how you might modify the performance review so you have the best chances of improving productivity and effectiveness in your work unit and for each of your employees. We'll concentrate on employees at three performance levels, but offer some suggestions on other employee differences you may encounter.

> **Different Employees ... Different Paths** Smart Managing
>
> For the employee review to have value, you have to be clear about what you want to achieve with each individual employee, taking into account where the employee is and where she or he can go. The review process needs to be customized to fit individual employee situations.

The Underperforming Employee

Managers are most comfortable reviewing the performance of employees who perform adequately or excel. That's understandable. Reviewing the underperforming employee is challenging, because there's always a possibility the employee will refuse to recognize or address performance issues and will act in unpleasant ways. Before we look at how you address under-performing employees, let's consider what you need to accomplish during the review process.

Your Goals

What do you want to achieve during the performance review when the employee is performing at a level that's lower than desirable? By the end of the performance review meeting, you want to have achieved the following in terms of *improving performance:*

- Identified areas where the employee needs improvement.
- Identified possible reasons for lower performance.
- Worked with the employee to identify solutions.
- Created an action plan to implement solutions and track results.
- Scheduled any formal, ongoing follow-ups and communication as needed.
- Created a written record (documentation) of the discussion.

These are your first-tier goals. In some situations, particularly with employees unwilling or unable to enter into the performance improvement process in good faith, you may have second-tier goals. These kick in when your concern shifts away from performance improvement to reducing or eliminating the impact of sub-standard performance. For example:

- Began (or completed) a process of progressive discipline to apply consequences for poor performance.
- Protected yourself and the company from unwarranted claims of discrimination or other illegal workplace practices.
- Minimized the negative effects of the employee's poor performance on the company or coworkers.

Two Different Situations

There are two distinctively different situations with respect to underperforming employees. They should be handled very differently. We're going to label these "minor underperformance" and "major underperformance."

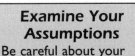

Examine Your Assumptions

Be careful about your assumptions regarding an employee's performance. If you assume an employee cannot improve, you will probably follow a path that ensures an employee won't improve and create a self-fulfilling prophecy. That can be costly.

Minor underperformance involves most of the following:

- Performance problems are a recent onset and not yet chronic.
- The impact of performance problems on the work unit is minor, but it may worsen.
- The employee appears to be willing to address issues and work to improve.
- The employee has succeeded in the job in the past *or* appears to have the ability to improve.

The key thing to remember with respect to minor underperformance is that it seems highly probable that performance problems can be fixed within a reasonable time and without investing huge resources to fix the problems.

On the other hand, major underperformance is such that the odds of fixing the performance problems are stacked against you (and the employee). Major underperformance involves most of the following:

- The problems are chronic; they've existed for a long time.
- The problems have not been fixed despite your efforts to work with the employee.
- The employee is unwilling to acknowledge/address performance problems.
- The problems have a major impact on the work unit, the employee's coworkers, and productivity.

- The problems need to be solved in the near or immediate future.
- The employee lacks the ability to improve and has no record of success.

There is no flawless, objective way to identify which performance problem situations are minor and which are major. For this reason you should always assume that underperformance is minor until you have firm evidence that it is not so. In other words, the default conclusion is that, with help, the employee can overcome current difficulties.

Dealing with Minor Underperformance

What's your primary target in terms of dealing with minor underperformance? It's simple. You want to work with the employee to develop and implement a strategy to eliminate performance problems before they become major problems. This is consistent with the theme of this book, which is that your performance review role, unless otherwise indicated, is to work *with* the employee as a performance improvement partner. That's because, when your concern is to improve performance, it's absolutely necessary that the employee perceive you as being on the same side as him or her and sharing common interests. You cannot usually improve performance when you take a power-based or threatening stance with employees. In fact, if you try to pressure employees to improve performance by "leaning on them," you're more likely to make performance problems worse.

So, when dealing with minor underperformance during the performance review meeting, follow the steps and guidelines we've mapped out in Chapter 7. If those steps do not eliminate the problem, then switch gears to a more forceful approach— the kind of approach you take with someone with major underperformance.

Dealing with Major Underperformance

It's one thing to work with an employee with minor performance problems when the employee is willing and it's reasonable to assume that working together can eliminate the problems. It's a completely different matter to address a situation where it's unlikely you can work with the employee to improve performance, because the problems have existed over a long time, are very serious, or are accompa-

> **Legal Advice**
>
> When faced with major underperformance and if you're considering a disciplinary process, be sure you understand any specific laws that may apply *and* any details of collective agreements that may affect your actions. In large companies, the best place to start is the human resources department. For a small business, a labor lawyer can help.

nied by strong resistance or denial by the employee.

For example, let's say you discover that Frank is stealing money from the company's petty cash. This is a serious offense, in fact serious enough that you are justified (and even wise) to move from a "We are going to solve this together" approach to a disciplinary approach that might result in the employee being fired. Similarly, if an employee has been underperforming over four or five years, despite your best efforts to work with him or her to improve, at some point you have to move away from trying to improve performance to minimizing or eliminating the problems unilaterally.

Perhaps the major difference between dealing with minor and major performance problems is that your focus shifts away from improving performance to minimizing or eliminating the impact of the problem. With a shift in perspective comes a shift in action. With minor problems you work with the employee, but with major problems, as we have described them, you operate more unilaterally and make decisions about consequences of past or continuing performance issues. For

> **Balancing Obligations**
>
> **Smart Managing**
>
> Effective managers balance two obligations—to look after the interests of their employees and act humanely and to protect the interests of the organization. Focus on *only* one or the other and you create a number of unpleasant side effects.

example, the ultimate consequence might be termination of employment. Other consequences might involve demotion or a cut in pay. Clearly those decisions usually cannot be made with employee and manager as equal participants in the decision. That doesn't mean your actions will be unnecessarily heavy-handed. Neither does it mean that you need to totally give up on an employee. Progressive discipline is the tool you use to address these tougher performance problems in a way that's gradual and fair.

Progressive Discipline

Progressive discipline is the process you use to define and apply consequences in situations where performance is sub-standard, for the purpose of making a last-ditch attempt to jolt the employee into improving performance *or* reducing or elimi-nating the negative impacts of substandard performance. Conse-quences range from minor to major. At the extreme end is termination (or per-haps legal action). At the moderate end, there are actions such as removing privileges or benefits (e.g. travel, training opportuni-ties). In the middle lies a

Progressive discipline A managerial tool that involves applying various consequences, tied to performance in a progressive way (from less signifi-cant to more significant), to encour-age employees to improve their per-formance *or* move the process along so that the impact of poor perform-ance is reduced or eliminated.

wide range of actions that may include suspension with or with-out pay, docking of pay (e.g., for unexcused absences), denial of merit increase, and demotion.

The less serious consequences are intended to do two things. First, defining and applying consequences for poor per-formance sends a clear message to the employee that you are serious about the performance problem. Some employees won't move to address their performance problems unless they under-stand that negative things will happen if they don't. Second, the less serious consequences are there to provide some incentives to move forward.

Here's how that works. Let's say that your work unit sends three employees each year to a professional conference. You might choose to withhold that benefit from someone who is chronically late meeting deadlines. This has the effect of taking something away that an employee wants, but you can also structure it so that the employee is rewarded next year if and when he meets his deadlines. So, as a consequence of poor performance, the employee doesn't go this year, and, as a positive consequence for improving, the employee gets to go next year.

The most severe consequences—firing and demotion—are designed to end the problem by removing the person from the job.

There are some simple principles you should apply to the progressive discipline process.

- Any disciplinary action you take must conform to the legal requirements in your location, which includes local laws and contractual commitments.
- All disciplinary action must be documented in as much detail as possible. Documentation should include the nature of the performance problem (as specifically as possible), previous attempts to work with the employee to solve the problem, verification that the employee has been informed of potential consequences, any actions taken, and any results, positive or negative.
- Disciplinary action is based on the principle of "least possible force first." If necessary, more serious consequences and timelines can be imposed if less stringent ones don't bear fruit.
- Disciplinary action is appropriate only when you're absolutely sure the performance problems cannot be remedied by altering the environment, work system, or your management behavior, so as not to penalize an employee for things that are not under his or her control.

- The harsher the consequences you use and the more force you use, the less likely you will be able to re-create a positive relationship in the future with an employee. In other words, the more force, the less likely you can go back to more cooperative methods.

So, what does progressive discipline look like? The steps aren't complicated at all. They involve the following:

- Deciding on negative and positive consequences
- Communicating them to the employee
- Monitoring performance
- Applying the consequences
- Repeating the cycle as necessary, with more serious consequences

Let's walk through a progressive discipline scenario.

Here's the situation. Janet works as a customer support specialist. Her responsibilities include direct contact with customers, answering questions on the phone and in person, and developing better methods for tracking customer contact details and statistics and reporting customer information to her manager, Mary.

After a relatively slow decline in quality and quantity of work, the last three months have brought a rather sudden and extreme drop in Janet's work. Mary has been trying to work with Janet over time to bring her performance up to standard, coaching her and using an ongoing communication process. Part of that process was using performance diagnosis techniques to determine the source of the problems and Mary has been able to rule out causes in the system. She's fairly sure that, whatever the causes of the problem, they lie with Janet and not anywhere else. Unfortunately, despite these efforts, Janet's work has not improved and it seems like she has become more aggressive toward her manager, customers, and colleagues. It's now performance review time, and Mary has decided that a more active approach is needed, so she is initiating the progressive discipline process.

Here's part of the discussion.

Mary (after summarizing performance concerns that she has communicated to Janet throughout the year): Janet, it seems to me we still have some issues we have to deal with. I'm still getting customer complaints about the way you handle calls, and your monthly statistical reports have been incomplete and late each of the last three months. What's your take on what might be going on? (This is a final attempt to elicit Janet's cooperation to improve.)

Janet (curtly): Well, Mary, I don't see a problem. Everyone is getting complaints and it's not my fault if our customers are short-tempered. As for the reports, there's nothing I can do....There's not enough time in the day.... (She offers a number of excuses and generally continues to resist.)

Mary: Janet, we really need to get things on track here. We rely on you to ... (She outlines the areas where Janet's performance is substandard.) ... because you play an important role in keeping our customers happy. As you know, we have to decide on whether you will be receiving your annual merit increase and, at the moment, I can't recommend that you receive it, based on the problems we've talked about over the last months.

Here's what I want to do, and I think this is the fairest way to deal with the problem. I'm going to withhold the merit increase right now. But, that doesn't mean you can't get yourself up to standard and receive the increase during the next months. Once each month, I want to meet with you to go over how things have gone during the month. We'll go over your report for the month, which needs to be complete and available on time, and we need to review your customer interactions. If you get things done on time, and reduce customer complaints to (specific complaint level) for a period of three months, I'll make sure you receive your merit increase. (Notice that Mary is applying a consequence and providing an incentive to encourage Mary to upgrade.) However, if, by June, you have

Getting Agreement

While progressive discipline means that the manager defines consequences and then applies them, it's sometimes worth the effort to try to get the employee to agree that those actions are fair or even to involve the employee in defining consequences that seem reasonable to him or her. When that's possible, it greases the wheels, although it's not always possible.

not been able to bring up your performance, we're going to have to look at other options. We're not at the point where we need to think about putting you in a position with less responsibility or putting you on probation, and I'm sure neither of us wants to get to that point. If we can't make progress in the next few months, though, we're going to have to consider those options. Meanwhile, I'm willing to do everything I can to help you hit your targets. I know this situation has to be upsetting for you; it is for me. So how do you feel about this?

Janet (obviously upset): I'm getting tired of you picking on me. You have the power to do what you want, but I don't like it. (She makes some other comments that indicate anger and resistance.)

Mary: Janet, it's clear you're upset right now, and I can understand that. As I said, if we do this properly, I don't see any reason why we can't resolve these problems. Right now, here's what we need to do. I am going to record the details of our conversation, and that will include what you need to achieve over the next months to receive your merit increase and get things back on track. I'm going to ask you to read it and indicate that you've read it by signing it. Signing doesn't mean you agree with the contents, though, and you can add your own comments to the sheet. It's just a temporary record, and if your performance comes up to standard, the document can be removed from the file. We won't do that right now, though. I need a few days, and you need to think about this a bit too. So, I'll get the summary to you by Friday, and I'd like it back by the following Wednesday.

It's quite possible that Janet will remain uncooperative during the rest of the meeting and continue her substandard performance over the next few months. During and around the meeting, Mary needs to get across the idea that there are clear positive consequences for improving performance

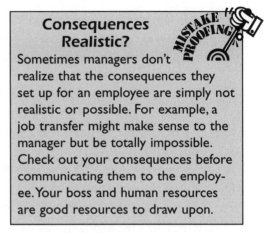

Consequences Realistic?

Sometimes managers don't realize that the consequences they set up for an employee are simply not realistic or possible. For example, a job transfer might make sense to the manager but be totally impossible. Check out your consequences before communicating them to the employee. Your boss and human resources are good resources to draw upon.

and clear negative consequences for failing to do so. She needn't do that in a harsh, personally attacking manner. She needs to do it in a calm but firm way that provides for clear measurable targets and ongoing help.

So what happens if Janet doesn't improve her performance? Mary has laid the groundwork to escalate the negative consequences for noncompliance. So, as agreed, at the next review meeting (a special, three-month interim review), the process is repeated.

If performance hasn't improved, Mary would probably put Janet on probation. Then, if performance doesn't improve within the term of probation, she would terminate or transfer her.

If Janet responds positively, then she receives the rewards promised and Mary would expect that the problems have been resolved. At the next year-end review, Mary would really emphasize the positive changes, apply any positive consequences, and remove any adverse comments from the permanent record.

Things to Remember About Progressive Discipline

In the scenario we just looked at, the attempts to identify and diagnose Janet's performance problems and Mary's efforts to work with her to improve performance extended over a fair amount of time, as did the progressive discipline process. In the example, Mary can afford to take her time. While the perform-ance problems need to be taken seriously, it's not absolutely necessary that they be resolved immediately.

However, to the extent that performance problems are more urgent, the helping process and the progressive discipline process can be and need to be accelerated. For example, if Janet's poor performance created safety hazards for other employees, the entire process could be condensed into a matter of weeks or even less. So, the speed at which you move to the disciplinary process and through it depends on the situation. The more urgent the situation, the faster you move.

There's an important question we need to address: "Why should you give the employee multiple chances?" It's true that you could move very quickly with employees who are under-performing. You could skip the progressive process, give the employee reasonable warning, and then invoke a severe conse-quence (e.g. firing) in a short time.

The most compelling reason to move more slowly is that when you get to the point where you have to apply severe puni-tive consequences, you've reached a situation where everyone has already lost. If you terminate an employee, you incur some very real costs. The cost of replacing an employee (recruiting, interviewing, orientation) is conservatively estimated at about 50% of the salary for that position. That doesn't include lost pro-ductivity as the new hire is getting up to speed—a period that can last as long as 12 months. On top of the replacement and productivity issues, there may also be termination settlements involved. Firing an employee may be necessary in some situa-tions, but it's not the solution of choice, because it's costly.

What about moving to strong consequences as quickly as possible? Why not place an employee on probation as soon as possible when performance problems occur? Why waste time working with an employee when it's not likely that he or she can be "rehabilitated"? That's a good question. The reason is that the stronger the consequences you use, the less likely the employee will turn his or her performance around. That's because strong consequences have an unfortunate side effect. They polarize the situation, creating an antagonistic relationship between manager and employee. Even if the employee improves, he or she may forever operate in antagonistic ways toward you, the manager who is perceived as the source of his or her problems. So, it seems logical that you would use strong negative consequences only as the strategy of last resort.

The Performing Employee

Thankfully, the large majority of employees are between the underperforming group and the excellent group. Performing employees are those who do not call special attention to themselves through their obvious failures or through very obvious successes. They chug along, doing their jobs somewhat imperfectly, with lots of room for improvement, given the proper circumstances. They are the most ignored group in terms of management time—and particularly the time managers spend in performance reviews.

That's unfortunate, because employees in this middle group are critical to improving your work unit's performance, because you can help them improve without investing huge resources. Also, when you do not pay much attention to these employees, some of them will tend to perform more marginally over time. So, the middle group may be where you can have the most impact. Ignore them and some will become poor performers. Pay attention and you can help some of them become excellent performers.

Your Goals

What do you want to achieve during your performance review meetings with employees who are neither excelling nor underperforming? By the conclusion of the meeting, you will have:

- Identified areas where performance improvement is possible.
- Completed the diagnostic process and developed strategies

to improve performance, which may include training, changes in the work environment, and assistance from you.
- Identified the areas in which the employee is succeeding and focused on them so the employee knows you recognize his or her accomplishments.
- Provided any incentives for the employee for specific improvements.

We've mapped out the elements of the performance review in Chapter 7; those are the steps you will be following. In most cases, it shouldn't be necessary to use progressive discipline with a middle-performing employee. If there's a central theme to follow with these employees, it's to continue to work with them and to focus on continual improvement. Work to stretch the employee: ask just a little more from him or her, while recognizing what's going well.

The Excellent Employee

Managers tend to spend far less time and energy reviewing the performance of excellent employees. On the surface of it, it makes sense. After all, why bother spending time discussing performance with employees who are doing very well, when others who perform less well might benefit from that extra time?

The answer is simple. If you ignore your excellent employees, you risk either losing them completely or having their performance drop to average levels. All employees have needs—things that will help them maintain their performance, motivation levels, and skill levels. When you neglect those needs, you risk damaging your most valuable resources—the great performers. In particular, your excellent performers need to have their achievements recognized and need to have challenges and opportunities to grow. If you don't provide recognition, challenges, and growth opportunities, some of your best employees will look elsewhere for job satisfaction and you may lose them. Or, as boredom sets in and the work becomes more and more routine, their performance will fall.

Here's another thing to keep in mind. Excellent employees have more job options than poor employees. Since they're so skilled and effective, they're more likely to leave for more challenging positions in other companies. They also tend to have relatively high levels of confidence in their abilities and may be more willing to leave your organization. If you want to keep your excellent performers, you need to pay attention to them—and the performance review process is an important tool.

> **Providing Challenges** 🎩 *TRICKS OF THE TRADE*
>
> Tangible rewards (money, recognition) can play important roles in keeping your excellent performers performing at high levels. However, it may be *more* important to focus on providing challenges, stimulating your excellent employees, and offering career development opportunities. Job boredom is a significant contributor to the loss of good employees.

Your Goals

The performance improvement goals we suggested for underperforming employeea can be relevant to even the excellent employee, since it's always possible for anyone to improve, regardless of the current level. So, you can look for areas where an excellent employee can improve, and you can identify and diagnose barriers to his or her performance. Don't neglect this part.

However, in addition to those goals, you can "go different places" with the excellent employee. For example, you can use his or her insights and expertise to help you improve the system of work for everyone or you can identify why he or she is excelling so you can teach other employees the "secrets" of better performance. In other words, you can learn useful things from the excellent employees that you might not be able to learn from the others.

So, here's where you should be at the end of the performance review meeting with the excellent employee. You want to have achieved the following:

- Identified what she or he does differently, so you can better help the other employees.

- Accumulated information about work system barriers he or she has identified.
- Administered any appropriate rewards or recognitions.
- Planned for and arranged for new job challenges.
- Identified development strategies to ready him or her for promotion.

Is there a central theme that applies to performance reviews with the excellent employee? Yes. You want to recognize their accomplishments, maximize their contributions, sometimes by moving them beyond the parameters of their jobs, and seek to enrich their work experiences so they are less likely to look for new challenges elsewhere.

Manager's Checklist for Chapter 11

❑ Conduct performance reviews in a flexible way that takes into account each employee's performance level (high, middle, average) and what is likely to work with him or her specifically.

❑ Use progressive discipline techniques, but only when you're sure that performance problems are not a result of factors in the work environment or with your own actions, so as not to penalize an employee for things beyond his or her control.

❑ First try working with employees in a helping, cooperative way to improve performance. Only if that fails should you become more unilateral.

❑ Don't ignore your middle or excellent performers. Spend time with them to make sure their performance improves or stays stable.

❑ Keep in mind that disciplinary action may be necessary but that it often has undesirable long-term side effects that make establishing a productive employee-manager relationship very difficult.

Facing Real-World Problems

M anagers tend to focus on the problems associated with performance reviews—the tough situations that they believe will result in unpleasant review meetings. That's not surprising since it's the "employees from hell" that cause managers to lie awake at night, particular around performance review time. The reality is that if you follow the principles and techniques we've outlined in this book, you'll find that the vast majority of performance reviews will go well and won't be unpleasant in the least.

There's a flip side, though. While we don't want to be looking for the worst, neither do we want to be naïve. You need to be prepared for some of the real world problems most managers face connected with the performance review process. That's what this chapter is about—to identify tough situations you *are* going to encounter and provide you with some tools to deal with them. We are going to start with the biggest real world problem you are likely to face—disagreements.

Managing Disagreements

Disagreements during the performance review *are* going to
occur. After all, we use imperfect methods to review and evaluate performance and then we make decisions based on those
imperfect tools. Given our imperfect tools and our own very
human imperfections, it shouldn't surprise us when there are
differences of opinion. How you manage those disagreements
will determine whether a productive relationship is created or
maintained between employee and manager or whether the
relationship takes on the characteristics of an all-out war. Many
a manager has botched disagreements and turned high performers into problem performers.

The first step in improving your ability to manage performance review disagreements is to recognize that they occur as a
natural and normal part of the process. So here's your first tip.
Don't assume that a disagreement is the "fault" of the employee. The reasoning is simple. When you attribute the cause of a
disagreement to the employee, you discount what might be
valuable information the employee may have to offer. The
blaming process polarizes
the situation, so you tend
to listen less and lose
good information.

> **Keep Your Mind Open**
> Start from the position that
> you and the employee disagree,
> *but* that there may be important,
> accurate truths in what the employee
> has to say. Treat your own position as
> most likely accurate, but not neces-
> sarily the "final word."

The second step is to
realize that disagreements
during performance
reviews do not always
have to be unpleasant or
destructive. In fact, the
opposite is possible. Disagreements, handled well, can improve
performance and productivity. Each disagreeing person may
have a different angle on an issue.

For example, Tom may attribute drops in his performance
to company cutbacks and higher workloads, while Beth, his
manager, may believe that Tom is not learning new and neces-

sary skills quickly enough. It could very well be that they need to address *both* causes to improve Tom's performance. The disagreement can result in a better strategy to improve performance than either Tom or Beth might generate on his or her own.

Principles of Disagreement Management

As you'll see in a moment, the way you manage disagreement during performance reviews will depend on the context and nature of the disagreement. Regardless of specifics, you can abide by some fundamental principles for managing disagreements.

- It's not always possible to eliminate a disagreement. Your goal is to manage the disagreement to maximize positive outcomes and minimize negative outcomes.
- The way you handle disagreement during the review is a critical determinant of whether the employee will continue to work with you over time.
- The more riding on a decision (and disagreement about the decision), the harder it is to manage disagreement. That's why some of the worst disagreements have to do with rewards and punishments or consequences.

Where the disagreement issue is not quite so important to the success of the work unit, be prepared to give in occasionally as a gesture of goodwill. Some fights are simply not worth fighting.

Power-Based Disagreement Management

As the manager, you have some degree of formal power that entitles you to make a unilateral decision when and if you and the employee reach an impasse and cannot work out a solution you can both live with. Note that you have *some* degree of power. Managers tend to overestimate their power, so watch out. However, even if it's possible to use the power you have to end a disagreement, you should use it as a last resort. Why?

The use of managerial power can create very serious problems in the future, because overuse damages the relationships

⚠ CAUTION!

Don't Jump into Using Power

It's tempting to use power to end disagreements because it's a much quicker path than negotiation. Don't use power as a knee-jerk response to disagreement. Always consider the possible short- *and* long-term consequences before deciding to use power.

needed to create a productive and effective organization. It can create an adversarial relationship that affects employee cooperation, involvement, and communication.

For example, if Beth and Tom disagree on the merit increase for the year and Beth uses her formal power to deny an increase, it's very probable that Tom may perceive the decision as unfair and react in ways that are not in anyone's interest. Tom's reactions to a power imposed "solution" may end up hurting his performance over the next several months or years.

When you use your formal power to address disagreements, you must be aware of the possible negative consequences and do so in a way that tends to minimize negative outcomes.

What's the bottom line on using power to address disagreement? First, you probably will need to use it, but it should only be used after other more cooperative avenues have been explored with the employee. Second, when you present a unilateral decision to "settle" a disagreement, explain your decision as fully and as rationally as possible. Saying, *"I'm the boss, and what I say goes"* isn't going to cut it. Here's something much better:

> Tom, I think we're not going to be able to agree on the merit increase, but here's what I'm going to do. I need to make a recommendation this week and I think, based on (recap performance issues), that I'll recommend that the merit increase be delayed and we'll re-examine the situation in three months. I know it's not what you were hoping for, but I think that's the fairest way to do things.

That brings us to the third point. If you make a unilateral, power-based position to address an intractable disagreement, give something away. That's what Beth is doing above. Even

though Tom hasn't even
mentioned the possibility
of an interim review, Beth
offers it up. This shows
that she is trying to be
open-minded and fair. Fair
is important. When
employees feel you're *trying* to be fair and you're
listening to their points of
view, they're much more

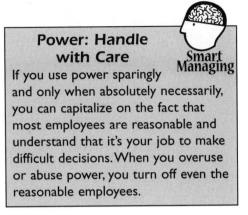

**Power: Handle
with Care**

Smart Managing

If you use power sparingly
and only when absolutely necessarily,
you can capitalize on the fact that
most employees are reasonable and
understand that it's your job to make
difficult decisions. When you overuse
or abuse power, you turn off even the
reasonable employees.

likely to cooperate, in the present and future, even though they
disagree with the decision.

Tips for Handling Disagreement Through Negotiation

If it's important to avoid unilateral, power-based approaches to
disagreement whenever possible, what does that leave? Negotiation and working with employees.

The skills needed to negotiate effectively can be quite complex. For this reason, if you're interested in improving those
skills, you might want to check out some of the negotiation
resources included in the bibliography at the back of the book.
However, we can still provide some tips, principles, and hints.

- Negotiation requires that both parties be committed to listening to each other and understanding each other's
  desires, needs, and perceptions. You can't force an
  employee to do that, but you can listen, not interrupt, and
  make a concerted effort to understand and communicate
  your desire to understand by using questioning and listening skills. (See Chapter 9.)
- To achieve some clarity and common understanding
  when negotiating, try to link your perceptions and opinions to concrete events or observations you may have
  made. So rather than saying, *"I think your communication skills are unacceptable,"* try *"I recall some instances*

where you were very argumentative in meetings, so let's look at that and how we should reflect that in our decisions."

- If you seem unwilling to be flexible in terms of the discussion and conclusions, the negotiation process will be a sham and look like a sham. Negotiations shouldn't be used as window-dressing for an autocratic decision you've already made.

- It's important to have a sense of what compromises you can make and what you absolutely need from the negotiation process before you start the process. It's also good for the employee to have an opportunity to think about those issues for himself or herself. In situations where unexpected disagreements occur, it's often a good strategy to put that particular issue on hold for a few days and then return to it after both of you have had time to think about the issue more carefully.

- Negotiations work best when you have a preexisting relationship with the other person. If you haven't spoken to the employee for 12 months and expect to have effective negotiations, you'll be disappointed. Ongoing communication throughout the year creates the foundation needed for negotiation during reviews.

- If you hit an impasse, buy time. Take a break, move to another easier issue, or allow some time for both of you to reflect and think.

- Negotiations can be affected by momentum. To create positive momentum, consider tackling the disagreements you and the employee feel will be easiest to resolve. Once you create positive momentum by solving the easier ones, it's easier to solve the tough ones.

- Be aware that people sometimes get caught up in the competition or game of negotiating and focus far too much on winning. That's not your goal. Your goal is to find common ground you both can live with, while improving the long-term relationship between you and the

employee. If you can't commit to those goals, you probably aren't negotiating any more.

- It takes two to negotiate. If the employee has proven
  beyond a shadow of a doubt that he or she is unwilling to
  negotiate in good faith, then it makes sense to fall back
  on a power-based solution. However, allow the employee
  some time to alter his or her approach to negotiating
  before concluding it's a dry hole.

Addressing Biases and Increasing Evaluation Accuracy

If you are in the position of using performance review results to
evaluate employee performance for the purpose of allocating
rewards, incentives, and negative consequences, you need to be
concerned with the accuracy of your evaluations. If evaluation
conclusions are inaccurate, there's a serious possibility that
employees will come to see
the process as unfair,
whether the inaccuracies
relate to them personally or
whether they relate to evaluations, rewards, and consequences for *other*
employees.

Of course, gross inac-
curacies in employee
assessment can result in
gross errors in any deci-
sion-making based on

> **Employees Are Watching** ⚠ CAUTION!
>
> Employees assess your
> fairness and accuracy in two ways.
> They look at how you treat them and
> they look at how you treat their col-
> leagues. Keep in mind that your biases
> and any inaccuracies you introduce
> into a single employee's performance
> review are likely to affect the percep-
> tions of other employees.

those assessments. One of the major contributors to inaccuracy
in evaluation is something called *evaluation bias*. You may not
have considered bias, since its effects are often hidden and
insidious.

Evaluation bias doesn't just refer to the obvious biases that
occur when you might like or dislike an employee. Evaluation

> **Key Term**
>
> **Evaluation bias**
> Common tendencies to make inaccurate evaluation judgments as a result of factors completely unrelated to the actual performance of the employee.

bias refers to common and almost universal tendencies that affect people when they evaluate anything and that cause those evaluations to be inaccurate. Here's a list of these tendencies that can skew your evaluations:

- **Halo effect**—the tendency to evaluate someone more positively in all categories because he or she is high in one or two areas.
- **Devil effect**—the tendency to evaluate someone negatively across the board because he or she is underperforming in one or two areas.
- **Recency effect**—the tendency to evaluate (either more positively or more negatively) based on events that have occurred more recently, rather than considering events occurring during the entire evaluation period.
- **Central tendency effect**—the tendency to evaluate in the middle, to judge most employees as being average even in situations where they are excelling—most prevalent in rating systems and scales.
- **Leniency bias**—the tendency to evaluate higher than is warranted, usually accompanied by some rationalization as to why this is appropriate (e.g., "He had personal problems" or "She's had some bad luck").
- **Severity bias**—the tendency to evaluate lower than is warranted, the opposite of leniency bias.
- **Opportunity bias**—the tendency to credit or blame the employee and ignore the reality that opportunity (factors beyond the control of the employee) may either restrict or facilitate performance.
- **False attribution errors**—the tendency to misattribute success and failure and assume they are both under the complete control of the employee when they often are not.

Countering Bias

The best way to counter the effects of various biases is to be aware of their influence and make conscious efforts to minimize their effects. Here are some suggestions.

A day or two after the review meeting and before you and the employee finalize the results of the review, reexamine any conclusions, ratings, and assessments in light of possible bias. For example, to counter possible recency bias, ask yourself, "Have we focused too much on the last few months rather than the entire period?" Or, for central tendency bias, ask yourself, "Are most of my employee reviews resulting in assessments clustered around the middle? If so, has my tendency to do that affected this particular employee's results?"

As we've indicated earlier, reviews are done with the employee. When you and the employee are relatively equal partners in the review process, each of you serves as a counterbalance to the other. The employee may be influenced by a particular bias and you may be influenced by other biases. Biases are easier to spot by someone other than the person being influenced by them.

Document and communicate throughout the review period, so performance-related information for the entire period is collected as it emerges. Notes and any documentation from the entire review period help you balance the very common tendency to review based on recent events.

Improving Evaluation Accuracy

If you follow the procedures outlined in this book, your review results are more likely to be more accurate. Keep in mind, though, that no evaluation can be flawless and accurate, because our measurement tools are often not accurate or flawless.

The most effective way to improve accuracy is to do proper performance planning and set measurable goals and objectives you and the employee can use during the review to determine whether performance has hit or exceeded the target. However, there are trade-offs and caveats. The more measurable a goal

Smart Managing

Perfect Accuracy?

Accuracy is very important in performance reviews, but perfect accuracy is a little like the quest for the holy grail. It might exist, but getting to it might be so difficult that it's not worth trying. Work to be as accurate as possible, but keep in mind that achieving perfection may be impossible or at least not worth the effort.

or objective, the more likely it is to be trivial with respect to the employee's contributions, because it's often the hardest to measure functions that are most important. Also, when you strive for greater accuracy, you need a larger number of measurable objectives to properly cover the breadth of an employee's performance. Measurable objectives are, by their very nature, quite narrow, so you need more than if your objectives were less measurable.

The degree to which you strive for accuracy will depend on your particular context and, in particular, the job tasks of the employee. Some tasks are easy to measure accurately and meaningfully. A good example would be "total sales for the review period." It's easy to determine and it's objective and it's important for gauging a salesperson's success. On the other hand, if you want to evaluate an employee's contributions to his or her team, that's much harder to measure, but may be important. Then there are the tasks that are easy to measure but not so important. For example, you can measure the total calls handled by an employee in a call center in a given period. That won't tell you about the *quality* of the interactions between the customers and the employee, something that's far more important than the number of calls.

The bottom line is that you need to choose what's important and evaluate the costs and benefits of creating measurable objectives. It's probably best to err on the side of conservatism and use enough objective measurable goals so that you cover at least 80% of the employee's major job responsibilities.

The Soft Stuff Dilemma

One of the areas where confusion abounds is in addressing the so-called "soft stuff" of performance. "Soft stuff" refers to very important things like communication, leadership, creativity, and teamwork. Most people intuitively realize that we can't ignore those things, because they *are* important aspects of performance for many jobs.

Here's the challenge. The "soft stuff" areas are where you're most likely to encounter very strong resistance from employees. You may find that employees who are comfortable acknowledging that their sales or production outputs have dropped will not be comfortable hearing that their leadership performance has dropped. That's because observations about a person's ability to communicate are much more personal and subjective than, let's say, an observation that their sales have dropped 10% in the last year. Employees may not be happy about drops in sales figures, but they see comments about their teamwork, leadership, and communication as exceedingly personal.

So the dilemma about addressing the "soft stuff" in reviews is this: if you do, you risk probing sensitive areas, but if you don't, you undoubtedly miss out on very important positive and negative contributions by the employee.

Couple that dilemma with the fact that rating systems that reference "soft stuff" are often used with almost no suggestions to help employee and manager understand "soft stuff" in similar ways and an employee is likely to react with bad feelings and resistance to even acknowledging "soft" skills that he or she needs to develop. Rating systems that are vague are almost guaranteed to stumble even more in these softer areas.

You probably can't afford to ignore "soft" contributions during reviews. Over the years, employees have become less isolated, and more interconnected with their colleagues, teams, and other people, making "soft" areas much more important. A highly productive factory worker, for example, may be so per-

> ### ⚠️ CAUTION! ⚠️ Don't Assume a Common Understanding
> People understand in different ways what leadership, creativity, teamwork, and other "soft" skills actually mean in terms of behavior and outcomes. Don't assume you and the employee understand the meaning of these words in the same way. Before evaluating an employee on a specific "soft" item, discuss with him or her what the item means to each of you.

sonally disruptive to colleagues that any contributions he brings to the organization are negated by his effect on the productivity of others.

What to Do

Are there ways to address "soft" areas to reduce the chances of stirring up bad feelings during the review? Yes.

First, the more the manager and the employee share common understandings of what the employee will be held accountable for, the less likely problems will come up when they review the "soft stuff." There are two points of impact to address. First, during performance planning, pay special attention to making sure that you and the employee have discussed and agreed on the criteria used to assess "communication with customers," "team contributions," or other important "soft" areas of contribution. Second, at the review meeting, you and the employee should discuss those criteria again before reviewing contributions in a specific "soft" area. This is particularly important if you're required to use very vague rating systems to assess these "soft" areas.

Take a look at the following dialogue to see how this might work with such a rating system.

Manager: John, on the form we need to decide on a rating that fairly reflects your ability to contribute to your work team. If you recall, when we met to plan for the year, we identified some indicators that would tell us your contributions could be assessed as "superior." Before we look at those, what does this item mean to you now?

Employee: Well, as I recall, we talked about some of the things I could do during team meetings to contribute more effectively, like encouraging more silent team members to talk and reducing my interruptions.

Manager: Yes, that's what I remember too. Let's start with those. How do you think you've done in terms of those indicators?

The conversation proceeds along those lines and, ideally, the manager and the employee reach agreement. What's important here is that there's at least *something* that both manager and employee can use as indicators of success or failure. If they disagree, at least the manager has some concrete instances to point to. For example, *"John, I do recall several meetings in June and July where you were arguing quite strenuously and not letting others complete their points."*

Finally, it's possible to focus on the *results* of good communication or teamwork rather than on whether the employee "has good communication skills" or "has good leadership skills." We want to move away from character traits to either behavior or outcomes that show those traits.

Here's an example. We don't want to evaluate an employee on creativity, because that's a very personal attribute. However, we can translate that trait into behaviors or outcomes that will indicate that the employee is being creative on the job. We could do it this way: "Developed two new product ideas" or "Contributed innovative cost cutting measures yielding 15% cuts in overhead." This approach can be used both during performance planning and in performance reviews. In the former, the behaviors or outcomes would be phrased as future-oriented goals. In the latter, they could be used as observations to support a particular rating. In both cases the analysis moves toward concrete, easily understood indicators.

Getting from Bad to Better Systems

OK, now, you've almost finished this book. Let's say that you want to improve a performance review system that's not been working well. Let's assume that you have a fairly clear idea

Smart Managing

Overcoming Cynicism

Most employees have been through several cycles of "Here's our brand-new performance management system and it's the best thing since sliced bread" talk, only to realize it's the same old thing in different clothing. You must consider this cynicism, be patient, and prove to employees that the changes made are real changes, in substance, not just appearance.

about how you want to change the performance management and review process. What's the best way to make the changes so you can see the benefits quickly?

The major stumbling block in improving a poor system isn't necessarily about making changes in procedures or the nuts and bolts of the review process. It's in getting the confidence of employees so they believe the new way will indeed be different from the former, bad way. This is because performance reviews are going to be valuable only if the employee and manager can work together and the goals of performance review are clearly to improve performance rather than to find fault or punish. Here are some tips.

First, the time to introduce a new and improved performance review system is *not* just before the reviews take place. The best time is during the performance planning stage, which might be as far as one year away from the review meetings—because that's really the starting point for the performance review/management process.

Before you begin the new cycle of planning, communication, and review, explain to employees how you want to change things and how the goals of the process have changed. Give them an overview of the components—planning, ongoing communication and the performance review. At that point, involve them in the creation of the better process by asking them for feedback and suggestions on how to make the process work for them. Encourage them to be active participants.

That information in itself won't convince anyone things are going to change, but it's the starting point. What will turn the tide of skepticism is how you conduct the planning meetings and how you manage communication throughout the year. When employees see your behavior change—when you alter your communication, for example—then and only then will they begin to climb on board. By the performance review meeting phase, most employees will be much more open and supportive of the changes—provided they've seen these changes. They'll also be more willing to work with you during the review meetings.

The final step in gaining employee commitment to the new process is directly related to your ability to manage the performance review meeting in a different and much more meaningful way than before. It's when you "walk the talk" that you prove to employees that things will be better and that it's worth cooperating and actively participating in this new system.

A Really Poor Review System

As a manager, you have control over some aspects of the performance review process. You are the one responsible for building good relationships, communicating effectively, deciding on the best ways to plan performance, and other factors that determine whether your review process is going to be worthwhile or not. But, and it's a fairly big "but," you don't control what your organization requires of you in terms of completing forms or following a rigid format and/or time sequence for reviews. Sadly, probably about 50% of organizations either provide *no* guidance and help to managers or require managers and employees to use a system that is flat-out terrible.

Now that you've gone through this book, you should have a good idea of what works and what doesn't and how you can conduct performance reviews so the process is no longer unbearable and so it helps everyone succeed. But what if your company forces you to do things that are in direct contradiction with what we know about how to make performance reviews successful? It's not an ideal situation, but you can rescue the process.

If you're required to use a poor system, then certainly you should lobby human resources or whoever is foisting the poor system on you to change it or, at minimum, to allow more flexibility in how managers conduct the performance review and performance management process. You may be surprised to find that the decision-makers in your company may be willing to make changes, because they've already realized that their current system isn't working. On the other hand, you may find them completely unwilling to change or allow flexibility.

Before we get to specifics about what you can do in the latter situation, consider this. The company may dictate a formal system of performance review that managers must follow. For example, it may require you to complete a specific form on a specific date. It may require you to use some sort of 360-degree software system or other technological solution. The important point is that the system you're obligated to use probably prescribes the *minimum* things you need to do. It doesn't necessarily mean you can't add components in an informal way. That's how you reduce problems that arise in a poor system.

> **TRICKS OF THE TRADE**
>
> **Augment!**
>
> The key to making a poor system work is to augment it. There's no reason you can't customize the interpersonal side of reviews and add documentation or procedures to improve it. A good manager makes a poor system work by focusing on the communication aspects of the entire review process.

Your employer may require you to submit a completed rating form for each employee every April. Let's say the form is a disaster: it confuses you and the employee and almost always contributes to really bitter disagreements between you and your employees. Other managers simply conform to the requirements and then live with the negative outcomes, poor employee relations, and lost productivity. The savvy manager, in contrast, doesn't rely on the form to make the process work.

If you have to submit a completed version of a poorly designed form, then submit it. That doesn't mean you can't add a performance planning process to what you do. It doesn't mean that you have to restrict performance documentation to *only* that specific form. It doesn't mean you can't communicate with employees throughout the year. After all, the company isn't telling you *not* to do things; it's simply telling you the minimum you need to do.

There are two things to keep in mind here. There's a tendency to view time spent doing more than necessary for reviews as time spent badly. That's an extremely shortsighted viewpoint that managers adopt because of their experiences with really poor review procedures. Once you realize how you, your employees, and the company can benefit when you invest more time than the minimum, you'll see that it's really in your best interests to allocate that extra time. Even if you haven't yet experienced the benefits you'll receive from doing extra, try it anyway. If you're skeptical, at least try to do things correctly to see if you believe it's worth it. Don't allow the poor system provided to you to convince you that the whole process has to be a waste of time. You'll be pleasantly surprised at the power of performance reviews to prevent and solve all sorts of problems.

Manager's Checklist for Chapter 12

❑ Disagreements during reviews are not always negative and don't have to be destructive. The way you handle disagreements determines whether the outcomes will be positive or negative.

❑ When dealing with disagreements about performance, the use of power should usually be a last resort, because of its possible long-term negative consequences.

❑ Bias in evaluation is something that happens with all of us. By being aware of your possible biases, you can evaluate your employees more accurately. If you do your evaluation of each employee in cooperation with him or her, you can tend to counterbalance each other's biases.

❑ It's often important to measure the "softer" areas of performance—leadership, creativity, teamwork, communication. It's best to try to translate those general areas into specific behaviors or indicators, so you and the employee share understandings of what those words mean.

❏ When you introduce a better, newly improved system, you must be prepared for employees to be cynical. When they realize the new system is truly different and better, they will embrace it. But you need to walk the talk.

❏ If you have to work within a poor review system that's thrust upon you, you can still make it work by adding components and relying on your interpersonal skills. The key is to augment what's required of you.

Appendix

Resources for Performance Reviews

Books

Arredondo, Lani, *Communicating Effectively* (Briefcase Books), McGraw-Hill, 2000
This discussion of the communication process and communication skills is written specifically for managers and supervisors.

Bacal, Robert, *Performance Management* (Briefcase Books), McGraw-Hill, 1999
This book provides in-depth help on the entire process of performance management, with broader coverage of the other parts of the performance management process.

Bacal, Robert, *The Complete Idiot's Guide to Dealing with Difficult Employees*, Alpha Books, 2000
This practical, hands-on book will help you deal with difficult employees, including information about disciplinary techniques and communication skills.

Bacal, Robert, *A Critique of Performance Management Systems—Why They Don't Work*, Bacal & Associates, 1998
This short discussion of the most common reasons why performance management and review systems fail badly presents an argument for more flexible, employee-involving alternatives. Available at http://work911.com/products or through Amazon.com.

Cohen, Stephen P., *Negotiating Skills for Managers* (Briefcase Books), McGraw-Hill, 2002
Negotiating is an important part of the review process. This book helps you improve your negotiating skills.

Max, Douglas, and Robert Bacal, *Perfect Phrases for Performance Reviews: Hundreds of Ready-to-Use Phrases That Describe Your Employees' Performance*, McGraw-Hill, 2003
This large collection of phrases can help you during the performance review process to describe employee performance at various levels from excellent to poor.

Tools

Bacal, Robert, *Performance Management Master Checklist Help Card*, Bacal & Associates, 2002
This checklist can be used to ensure you don't miss any steps in the performance review process. Available at http://work911.com/products. Free preview.

Bacal, Robert, *Performance Appraisal for Managers Help Card*, Bacal & Associates, 2002
This card summarizes the steps in the appraisal process, with dozens of tips and hints. Available at http://work911.com/products. Free preview.

Bacal, Robert, *Getting the Most from Performance Appraisal for Employees Help Card*, Bacal & Associates, 2002
Written for employees, this card can help employees understand the purposes and benefits of the review process, and how get the most out of it. Available at http://work911.com/products. Free preview.

Free Internet Resources

Performance Management and Appraisal Help Center
www.performance-appraisals.org
This free online resource contains hundreds of articles related to the performance management and review process and a free online forum where you can get help.

Performance Management and Appraisal Discussion List
groups.yahoo.com/group/perfmgt/
This e-mail discussion list for all aspects of performance management and reviews is a good place for you to offer help or to pose questions and get fast responses.

Work911 Electronic Newsletter
www.work911.com/newsletter.htm
Robert Bacal's free newsletter sends you free articles on a range of work-related topics, notifies you when new articles have been added to his sites, and announces and previews new Bacal books and tools.

Articles Indexing Directory Project
www.articles911.com
This online collection of the best work-related articles available on the Internet is not focused only on performance, but provides an ideal starting point for learning about other management issues.

Index

A

Accuracy in evaluation, 203-206
Action plans. *See also* Goals
  from feedback sessions, 149
  from performance planning
    meetings, 99
  from problem-solving meet-
    ings, 31-32
Active listening, 159, 160-161
Adversarial climate, 126
Anonymous feedback, 80-81
Appraisals, reviews versus, 10.
  See also Evaluation
Attention, conveying in body lan-
  guage, 161-162
Attitude, results versus, 14-15
Average, perceptions of, 64
Average performers, 193-194

B

Barriers
  to communication, 142
  to effective performance
    reviews, 18
  to performance, 5, 99, 129-
    133
Behavior
  as focus of feedback, 148
  performance versus, 41, 48
  personality versus, 14-15, 209
Biases, 203-205
Blaming
  with disagreements, 198
  eliminating, 127

problem solving versus, 11
Body language, 161-162
Bottom-line benefits of perform-
  ance reviews, 4, 7
Broad views of performance, 12-
  13, 40
Budgeting, 36-37

C

Central tendency effect, 204
Challenge, for top performers,
  194-195
Changes in job responsibilities,
  97, 108
Clarifying expectations, 105-108
Clarifying questions, 157-158
Clarity
  of definitions, 9-10
  of purpose, 7-9
  writing for, 151-152
Climate, adversarial, 126
Closed-ended questions, 155-157
Collaborative writing, 151
Collecting data, 28
Comments
  in computer-based review sys-
    tems, 85
  on rating forms, 58, 61, 115
Communication
  basic role in performance
    management, 23-26, 133-
    134
  costs of failure, 140-141
  feedback skills, 146-150